REGIONAL TRAMWAYS

WALES, ISLE OF MAN & IRELAND
POST 1945

REGIONAL TRAMWAYS

WALES, ISLE OF MAN & IRELAND
POST 1945

PETER WALLER

PEN & SWORD
TRANSPORT

AN IMPRINT OF PEN & SWORD BOOKS LTD.
YORKSHIRE – PHILADELPHIA

Regional Tramways: Wales, Isle of Man and Ireland

First published in Great Britain in 2018 by
Pen & Sword Transport
An imprint of Pen & Sword Books Ltd
Yorkshire - Philadelphia

ISBN 978 1 47386 190 9

Typeset in 11/13 Palatino by Aura Technology and Software services, India

Printed and bound in India by Replika Press Pvt. Ltd.

Pen & Sword Books Ltd incorporates the Imprints of Pen & Sword Books Archaeology, Atlas, Aviation,
Battleground, Discovery, Family History, History, Maritime, Military, Naval, Politics, Railways, Select,
Transport, True Crime, Fiction, Frontline Books, Leo Cooper, Praetorian Press, Seaforth Publishing,
Wharncliffe and White Owl.

For a complete list of Pen & Sword titles please contact

PEN & SWORD BOOKS LIMITED
47 Church Street, Barnsley, South Yorkshire, S70 2AS, England
E-mail: enquiries@pen-and-sword.co.uk
Website: www.pen-and-sword.co.uk

or

PEN AND SWORD BOOKS
1950 Lawrence Rd, Havertown, PA 19083, USA
E-mail: Uspen-and-sword@casematepublishers.com
Website: www.penandswordbooks.com

CONTENTS

Abbreviations 7

Preface 8

Introduction 9

BELFAST 53

BESSBROOK & NEWRY 67

CARDIFF 73

DOUGLAS 82

DUBLIN 96

FINTONA 108

GIANT'S CAUSEWAY 111

GREAT ORME 119

HILL OF HOWTH 124

LLANDUDNO & COLWYN BAY 130

LUAS 139

MANX ELECTRIC RAILWAY 144

SNAEFELL MOUNTAIN RAILWAY 162

SWANSEA & MUMBLES 169

PRESERVATION 175

Bibliography 181

ABBREVIATIONS

CIÉ	Córas Iompair Éireann
DUT	Dublin United Tramways
ERTCW	Electric Railway & Tramway Carriage Works
GNR(I)	Great Northern Railway (Ireland)
L&CBER	Llandudno & Colwyn Bay Electric Railway
M&G	Mountain & Gibson
M&T	Maley & Taunton
MER	Manx Electric Railway
NTM	National Tramway Museum
PAYE	Pay As You Enter
UDC	Urban District Council
UEC	United Electric Car Co Ltd, Preston
UTA	Ulster Transport Authority

KEY TO MAPS

Passenger lines
Lines closed before 1 January 1945
Non-passenger lines
Lines of neighbouring operators – open at 1 January 1945
Lines of neighbouring operators – closed at 1 January 1945
Passenger lines built opened after 1 January 1945
Lines under construction at 1 January 1945 – never completed

PREFACE

This is the fourth in a series that is intended, ultimately, to cover all the tramways of the British Isles. Its focus is primarily on those tramway systems in Ireland, the Isle of Man and Wales that operated after 1945. However, it also provides an overview of tramway development from the horse-tram era onwards. Following the introduction, there are individual chapters dealing with each of the first-generation tramways that survived into 1945 with a map that shows the system as it existed at 1 January 1945 and a fleet list of all the trams operated after that date. The volume also includes one second generation tramway – the LUAS system that operates around Dublin.

The majority of illustrations in the book are drawn from the collection of Online Transport Archive; in particular, I would like to express my gratitude to Barry Cross, John Meredith, the late Phil Tatt, Ian Wright – all of whose negatives or collections are now in the care of OTA – and the National Tramway Museum in whose care the collections of W.A. Camwell, D.W.K. Jones and R.B. Parr now reside. Martin Jenkins has been a great help in trying to track down certain images and providing comment. A number of individuals have also assisted with information; in particular I am grateful to the late John Gillham, the late Reg Ludgate, Peter Rowledge and Richard Wiseman. Every effort has been made to try and ensure complete accuracy; unfortunately, the records available are not always consistent and, with the passage of time, the number of those with detailed knowledge is unfortunately gradually declining. Likewise, every effort has been made to ensure the correct attribution of photographs. It goes without saying that any errors or fact or attribution are the author's and any corrections should be forwarded on to him care of the publishers.

A note on Welsh place names; where the names formed part of an historical company name, these have been left as originally spelt. Where the name forms part of the general narrative, the more usual spelling has been used – Llanelli rather than Llanelly, for example – except in the cases of Cardiff and Swansea where the traditional names have been used rather than Caerdydd and Abertawe.

Peter Waller,
Shrewsbury,
March 2017

INTRODUCTION

As each of the constituent parts of this volume were covered by separate legislation, the introduction is divided into four parts, covering Guernsey, Ireland, the Isle of Man and Wales.

GUERNSEY

The island of Guernsey, in the Channel Islands, is a Crown Dependency; not part of the United Kingdom but a remnant of the Duchy of Normandy. Although the island's defence and foreign affairs are controlled by the UK, its domestic laws are determined locally.

Following approval by the local authorities for its plans to construct a tramway from St Peter Port to St Sampson's, the Guernsey Steam Tramway Co was registered in London on 29 May 1878. The standard gauge, three-mile line opened with a fleet of two locomotives and six trailers on 6 June 1879. The fleet was expanded by a further four locomotives and one trailer in the early 1880s. The original company, however, failed, with operation ceasing in January 1889; its assets were acquired by the Guernsey Railway Co Ltd. Following reconditioning and the purchase of a further locomotive, the line reopened on 2 December 1889.

The new owners were keen to electrify the route and, employing Siemens as the contractor, electric operation commenced on 20 February 1892. Initially Siemens

One of the Guernsey Street Tramways original Merryweather locomotives of 1879 is pictured with fully-enclosed first-class carriage No 2 (built by Starbuck in 1879) and an open toast-rack car. The latter were nicknamed locally as umbrella cars. *Barry Cross Collection/Online Transport Archive*

July 11 1905

operated the electric services under contract whilst teething problems were ironed out; the company took over full operation in October 1893. Steam operation continued to supplement the initially erratic electric service and the final steam trams were withdrawn in the late 1890s. The electric trams, of which nineteen eventually saw service, were to survive through until 9 June 1934 when they were replaced by buses.

IRELAND

Following the Acts of Union of 1800/1, the whole island of Ireland formed part of the United Kingdom of Great Britain and Ireland until 1922. Although the construction of tramways in Great Britain was covered by the Tramways Act of 1870, powers for the building of tramways in Ireland

were covered by separate legislation – the Tramways (Ireland) Act of 1867 – although it was not until five years later that the first horse tramways to be constructed under the act were actually to open although the Dublin Tramways Co had a private Act in 1871.

The first horse tramway in Ireland predated the passing of the 1867 Act; the short line from Fintona to Fintona Junction was originally constructed under powers obtained in July 1845 by the Londonderry & Enniskillen Railway. The section of the company's line from Omagh to Fintona opened on 15 June 1853; however, the extension of the line southwards to Dromore Road, which opened on 16 January 1854, resulted in the diversion of the line away from Fintona, which ended up being at the terminus of a ¾-mile long branch from Fintona

Junction. In order to operate this short branch, the railway obtained powers from the Board of Trade to use a horse, although steam continued to be used for freight traffic. Operation of the line, which had been leased to the Dundalk & Enniskillen Railway (later the Irish North Western Railway) from 1 January 1860, passed to the Great Northern Railway (Ireland) on the creation of that company in 1876, although the Londonderry & Enniskillen Railway was not formally absorbed until 1883.

The first conventional street horse tramway in Ireland was that established by the Dublin Tramways Co, whose Act incorporated the powers from the earlier City of Dublin Tramways Co. The company opened its first 5ft 2³⁄₁₆in gauge line from College Green to Garville Avenue on 1 February 1872. The company's operations continued to expand and by the middle of the decade operated a fleet of 76 trams. A second operator in the city – the North Dublin Street Tramways Co – commenced operation of its first route on 10 December 1876, following powers obtained the previous year. In 1878 a third company – the Dublin Central Tramways Co – obtained powers to the south and south-west of the centre. Its first section opened on 17 March 1879.

The three tramway operators were all relatively small and on 1 January 1881 they merged to form the Dublin United Tramways Co; the new company possessed a network of 32 route miles,

A Dublin horse tram navigates the complex track at O'Connell bridge in the city centre. *Barry Cross Collection/Online Transport Archive*

Belfast City
Tramways horse tram
No 23 on a service to
Ligoniel. *Barry Cross
Collection/Online
Transport Archive*

half of which had been inherited from the Dublin Tramways Co. The new operator also acquired 137 horse trams and, as the network expanded, new trams were constructed between 1882 and 1896, both to supplement the older cars and to replace them. From 1897, the company commenced the conversion of its horse tram services to electric traction; the last horse cars operated in January 1901.

Alongside these operations, there was also the Dublin Southern District Tramways; this horse-operated 5ft 2³⁄₁₆in line opened from Haddington Road to Blackrock on 16 June 1879. This followed on from the opening of a disconnected section – from Dalkey to Kingstown – that was constructed to the 4ft 0in gauge and opened on 17 March 1879. The missing link between the two was connected on 9 July 1885 by the opening of the 5ft 2³⁄₁₆in gauge Blackrock & Kingston Co. In the early

1890s, the Dublin Southern sought powers to take over the Blackrock & Kingston, convert the 4ft 0in gauge section to 5ft 2³⁄₁₆in and to electrify the complete route. Dublin Southern electric services commenced on 16 May 1896.

On 10 August 1871, powers were obtained to operate horse trams in Belfast. The first section, from Castle Place to the Botanic Gardens, opened on 28 August 1872. The initial routes, all operated by the Belfast Street Tramways Co, were constructed to the 5ft 3in gauge, but in the late 1870s it was decided that future routes were to be built to the gauge of 4ft 9in and the existing routes converted to that gauge. There were three other concerns in the city that owned horse tramways – Sydenham District (opened 1888), Belfast & Ligoniel (opened 24 April 1893) and Belfast & County Down Railway (1894) – but these were all operated by the Belfast Street

Cork Tramways
Co No 6 is picture at the junction of Victoria Quay with Victoria Road in Cork. Nos 5 and 6 were slightly longer than the other four trams in the fleet, with eight, rather than six, windows longitudinally. *Barry Cross Collection/ Online Transport Archive*

Tramways Co. At its peak, the Belfast horse network extended over 33 route miles and employed 171 trams. On 1 January 1905, the operation of the tramway was taken over by the corporation and, following the completion of electrification work, the last horse trams operated in the city on 4 December 1905.

Although there had been proposals for an earlier horse tramway in Cork, it was not until 12 September 1872 that the Cork Tramways Co Ltd opened its route across the River Lee, linking Lower Glanmire Road station, at the end of Alfred Street, with Albert Street station on Albert Quay. The 5ft 3in gauge tramway was, however,

Two of the Warrenpoint & Rostrevor Tramway's 10 toast-rack trams, Nos 1 and 10, are pictured in Rostrevor. *Barry Cross Collection/Online Transport Archive*

unsuccessful and operation ceased in December 1875. The fleet's six cars were sold to the Dublin Tramways Co for further service.

The three-mile long 2ft 10in gauge Warrenpoint & Rostrevor Tramway was opened in 1877 to provide a link between Warrenpoint station and Rostrevor. Although the railway line was opened to Warrenpoint by the Newry, Warrenpoint & Rostrevor Railway in 1849, it never reached Rostrevor and the tramway built reflected 30 years of frustration in Rostrevor that the railway had never been extended. In all, thirteen single-deck horse trams were operated – ten toast-racks and three saloons – but competition from charabancs from 1907 made the line less successful financially. Final closure came in February 1915 as a result of damage to the track from a severe storm.

The 3ft 0in Galway & Salthill Tramway Co was established in 1877 to construct a link between the Midland Great Western station at Galway and Salthill, a distance of just over two miles. The line opened on 1 October 1879, with a fleet of five

double-deck cars supplied by Starbuck. A further two cars, this time single deck, were acquired in 1888. A batch of five new double-deck cars was acquired in 1909. However, the First World War was to see the line's demise as the tourist traffic, which represented a considerable portion of the line's income, declined whilst many of the company's horses were requisitioned for military use. The actual date of the line's closure is uncertain, but operation ceased in either 1918 or 1919.

Unusually, for Ireland, constructed to the British standard gauge of 4ft 8½in, the City of Derry Tramways was built to link the Graving Dock station of the Londonderry & Lough Swilly Railway and the Great Northern Railway (Ireland)'s terminus at Foyle Street. Until 1887 the Londonderry & Lough Swilly had operated – unofficially – over the lines of the Harbour Commissioners to Middle Quay, a mile south of the Graving Dock terminus. The City of Derry Tramways commenced operation on 1 April 1897 from Graving Dock station to the Fish Quay; it was extended to Carlisle Bridge later the

Galway & Salthill
No 3 heads out of Eyre Square into William Gate Street as it heads southwest towards Salthill. The impressive building in the background is the Railway Hotel adjacent to the Midland Great Western Railway station. *Barry Cross Collection/Online Transport Archive*

Two of the City of Derry Tramways Co's fleet are recorded passing on Shipquay Place on the system's sole tram route. *Barry Cross Collection/Online Transport Archive*

The passenger accommodation provided by the Glenanne & Loughgilly Tramway was somewhat rudimentary but the service was to survive for more than 10 years. *Barry Cross Collection/Online Transport Archive*

same year. Initially, the fleet comprised seven double-deck trams similar to those in operation in Belfast; with the conversion of the Belfast system, the company acquired a number of ex-Belfast trams to supplement its fleet. Never electrified, the City of Derry Tramways' horse trams ceased operation in January 1919.

A second horse tramway to commence operation in 1897 was the 1ft 10in gauge Glenanne & Loughgilly Tramway, which ran from Loughgilly station (known as Glenanne from 1924) through to Glenanne – a distance of about two miles. The tramway was owned by the linen mill owners George Gray & Sons and was used to convey both workers and finished goods. A single four-wheel covered car fitted with knifeboard seating was provided for passengers; services continued until 1919.

Although steam traction was originally used on the line to Fintona, this was in

the guise of a conventional railway and so the first steam tramway to operate in Ireland was the Dublin & Lucan Steam Tramway Co. This was authorised by an Order in Council in 1880 with construction starting at the end of that year. The first section of the seven-mile, 3ft 0in gauge tramway, from Dublin to Chapelizod, opened on 1 June 1881; it was extended to Palmerstown in November 1881 and through to Lucan on 20 February 1883. A separate company, the Lucan, Leixlip & Celbridge Steam Tramway Co was authorised to build an extension from Lucan; in the event only the 1½-mile section to Leixlip was completed. This opened in 1890 and was to survive through until closure at the end of October 1897. Steam operation of the line from Dublin to Lucan Spa Hotel ceased at some point in 1900 following a further Order in Council that permitted the electrification of the line and its conversion to 3ft 6in gauge.

Dublin & Lucan engine No 6 is seen at Ballydowd in 1895 at the head of a special school excursion heading into the Liffey Valley towards Lucan. *Barry Cross Collection/ Online Transport Archive*

Built to the 3ft 0in gauge, the line owned by the Portstewart Tramway Co was just over 1¾ miles in length and provided a connection between Cromore station, on the Belfast & Northern Counties Railways, and Portstewart. Although there had been earlier proposals, it was not until 28 June 1882 that the line commenced operation formally – actual services probably commenced a week or so earlier, prior to the line's inspection. Following financial failure, the line was acquired by the B&NCR in 1892 and thus passed to the Midland Railway in 1903 and to the LMS in 1923. Initially, two Kitson-built steam engines were supplied; these were later supplemented by further engines in 1883 and 1900. Operation of the line ceased on 30 January 1926. Two of the steam locomotives – No 1 of 1882 and No 2 of 1883 – were to be preserved after many years of storage in Belfast.

Authorised in 1881, the Cavehill & Whitewell Tramway was empowered to construct a three-mile line from the Chichester Park terminus of the Belfast Street Tramways in Cavehill through to the Glengormley Arms in Whitewell. The 4ft 8½in gauge line opened on 1 July 1882 with, initially, one Kitson-built steam locomotive. A further two locomotives were acquired in 1882 and 1886. Steam operation proved increasingly problematic with the result that, from 1892, horse traction was introduced and all steam services ceased four years later. Following a deal with BET, the line was electrified and the final horse trams operated in 1906.

Running from Victoria Bridge, on the GNR(I) line from Strabane to Omagh, the 7¼-mile long Castlederg & Victoria Bridge Tramway was authorised in 1883 and opened on 4 July 1884. The 3ft 0in gauge tramway was initially operated

In all, the Portstewart Tramway Co operated four steam engines all supplied by Kitson & Co of Leeds. One of the quartet is pictured with one of the two bogie trailers supplied by G.F. Milnes & Co of Birkenhead between 1897 and 1899 and the luggage van, No 3, that was new in 1882. *Barry Cross Collection/Online Transport Archive*

Dating from the early years of the Cavehill & Whitewell, this view records No 2 with one of the large open-top bogie trailers delivered in 1882. *Barry Cross Collection/Online Transport Archive*

The Castlederg & Victoria Bridge Tramway replaced its tram engines with more conventional steam locomotives. No 4 was built by Hudswell Clark and, after the line's closure, was to see further service on the Clogher Valley Railway. *Barry Cross Collection/Online Transport Archive*

One of the three of unusual double-cab 2-4-2Ts supplied by Thomas Green & Sons of Leeds between 1892 and 1906, No 10 (originally No 2 until renumbered in 1915), stands at the Terenure terminus of the Dublin & Blessington. A fourth of the type was supplied by Brush. *Barry Cross Collection/Online Transport Archive*

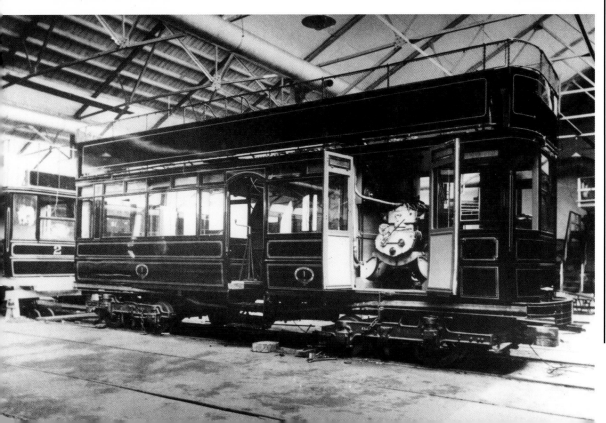

Dublin & Blessington Hurst Nelson petrol-electric Nos 1 and 2 were experimental cars delivered in 1915; the two were never successful. *Barry Cross Collection/Online Transport Archive*

by three Kitson-built tram engines; these were eventually replaced by conventional steam locomotives. There were four four-two-axle carriages built by Oldbury; these were supplemented after 1925 by a small petrol-engined railcar. Initially too light for service, the unit was subsequently rebuilt. As a result of strike action on the GNR (I) and on other railways in Northern Ireland, the last services over the line operated on 30 January 1933 and it was formally closed on 17 April 1933. A final train operated on 27 July 1934 when the rolling stock was transferred from Castlederg to Victoria Bridge for disposal. One of the four carriages, No 4 was rescued in the late twentieth century and has now been fully restored for display at Cultra.

The 5ft 3in gauge Dublin & Blessington Steam Tramway was authorised in 1887 to provide a connection from Terenure to Blessington. Services commenced on 1 August 1888 with six steam engines supplied by the Falcon

Works of Loughborough. These were later supplemented by four further locomotives – three supplied by Thomas Green & Son of Leeds and the other by Brush of Loughborough (the successor to the Falcon company) – that were of an unusual double-cab design. On 1 May 1895, the Blessington & Poulaphouca Steam Tramway was opened; this was operated by the Dublin & Blessington and, from 1896, through services from Terenure to Poulaphouca operated. The line beyond Blessington only was to survive until 1927. The rest closed in 1932.

In 1915, the company acquired two petrol-electric trams fitted with Aster petrol engines. Two later railcars were used between Jobstown and Terenure and were supplemented by a third railcar acquired from Drewry. Although there were plans for the line's partial electrification in 1911, these came to nothing largely as a result of the First World War. After the war,

A Clogher Valley Tramway service runs through the main street at Fivemiletown. The narrowness of the street and the presence of parked vehicles were to present a problem for the tramway in its later years. *Barry Cross Collection/ Online Transport Archive*

MAIN ST., FIVEMILETOWN.

the service faced increasing competition from buses and, despite efforts to see the line transferred to another operator, it was closed completely on 31 December 1932. Following closure, the Drewry and one of the smaller railcars were sold to the County Donegal Railway; the former was eventually to be preserved after having been converted to a trailer by the County Donegal.

Extending for some 37 miles from Tynan to Maguiresbridge, to the east of Enniskillen, the Clogher Valley Tramway was constructed following authorisation under the Tramways Act and followed the public highway for almost two-thirds of its distance. The 3ft 0in line opened throughout on 2 May 1887 and, seven years later, changed its legal status from tramway to railway. It was steam operated entirely until the delivery of a diesel railcar in 1932 and a diesel locomotive the following year; the former was

generally used on passenger services thereafter although steam was still used on some passenger when heavy traffic was expected. Financially, the line struggled and efforts to try and persuade the GNR(I) to take it over failed. It passed to a committee of management set up by the county councils of Fermanagh and Tyrone in 1928. The line finally closed over the night of 31 December 1941/1 January 1942. The 1932-built railcar was subsequently acquired by the County Donegal Railway and was preserved when that line closed.

The first electric tramway in Ireland – indeed one of the first in the world – was the 3ft 0in gauge Giant's Causeway, Portrush & Bush Valley Railway & Tramway Co. The line was promoted by Anthony and William Atcheson Traill following the failure of earlier plans to construct a steam tramway eastwards from Portrush along the coast to serve the world famous Giant's Causeway. Construction

Pictured before 1899 – notice the presence of the third rail alongside the track – Giant's Causeway saloon car No 4 hauls trailer No 10 westbound with Dunluce Castle in the background. *J. Joyce Collection/Online Transport Archive*

Giant's Causeway steam locomotive No 4, built in 1896, stands at Portrush with five trailers. In all the line possessed four steam locomotives. *Barry Cross Collection/ Online Transport Archive*

was authorised by an Act of 28 August 1880 and work started on construction on 21 September 1881. Although the intention was to use electric traction from the start, with Siemens being appointed technical engineers, the initial adoption of third rail power supply meant that the section through Portrush itself had to be steam operated. The line opened from Portrush to Bushmills on 29 January 1883 with steam operation for the entire length of the initial route; it was not until 28 September 1883, following completion of the hydro-electric station at Bushmills, that electric operation commenced. Passengers for Giant's Causeway were conveyed by horse bus from Bushmills. In 1885, the two-mile extension to Giant's Causeway was agreed; this opened on 1 July 1887. Following a fatal accident in 1895, in which a cyclist was killed, powers were obtained in 1896 to replace the exposed third rail with overhead; the conversion was completed on 26 July 1899. Although electric trams

could now operate through to Portrush station, the occasional use of steam continued through until the 1920s and the two steam locomotives were only disposed of in 1931. The interwar years proved difficult financially for the tramway but it was to survive and it proved invaluable during the war although it did suffer some damage – on one occasion a quarter of a mile of overhead was brought down by a trailing cable from a barrage balloon.

The Giant's Causeway line was the world's first hydro-electric powered tramway; the second was the Bessbrook & Newry Tramway. This line was proposed by the Richardson family, who owned the mills at Bessbrook, as a means of carrying coal and raw materials from Newry to the mills. When initially planned in 1881 the intention was to use steam with construction work commencing on 8 September 1883 of the three-mile 3ft 0in gauge line; however, on 26 May 1884, powers were obtained to use electricity with

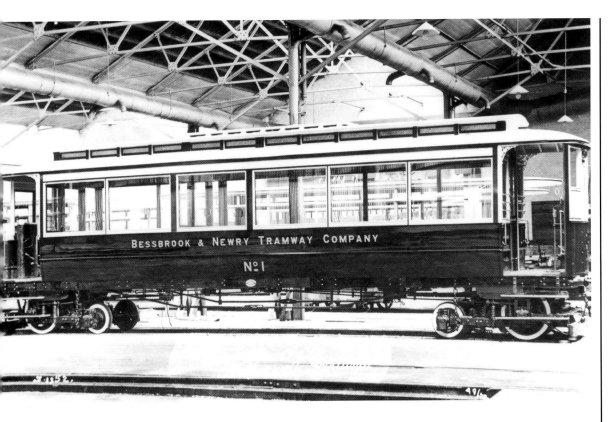

A maker's photograph portrays Bessbrook & Newry No 1 before delivery. This was one of two cars supplied by Hurst Nelson in 1920. *Barry Cross Collection/Online Transport Archive*

Three early Dublin electric trams portrayed in service on the Terenure route. Although all three were fitted with Peckham trucks, each came from a different body manufacturer: No 102 was built in the DUT's own workshops, No 168 was possibly imported from the USA and No 202 was built locally by Browne of Brunswick Street. All dated to around 1900. *Barry Cross Collection/Online Transport Archive*

The operation of electric tramcars by the Dublin Southern District Tramways was relatively short-lived – from May to September 1896 (when DUT took over) – but two of the Milnes-built cars are pictured here. In Dublin Southern operation, the cars bore the legend 'Dublin Electric Tramways' on their sides. *Barry Cross Collection/Online Transport Archive*

a hydro-electric plant being constructed at Millvale. Again, the third rail was adopted to provide the power except at road crossings where short sections of overhead were constructed. Following an inspection, the line opened on 1 October 1885. The Bessbrook & Newry also suffered in the immediate post-First World War years and there was a real threat of closure as the existing rolling stock required replacement. After some debate, agreement was reached between the government and the company to acquire new rolling stock provided that the former funded the upgrading to the line's generating equipment. As a result, a number of new and second-hand vehicles were acquired during the inter-war years. This ensured the line's survival through to

the outbreak of the Second World War and beyond.

The two tramway operators in Dublin – Dublin United Tramways and Dublin Southern District Tramways (a subsidiary of the Imperial Tramways Co) – merged to form the new Dublin United Tramways Co (1896). The DSDT had commenced operation of electric tramcars on 16 May 1896 and the final horse trams operated in the city on 13 January 1901. The DUT system grew to its maximum extent – 61 route miles – following the opening of the 5ft 2³⁄₁₆in gauge services over the erstwhile Dublin & Lucan line in 1928. There was a minor abandonment in 1932. Conversion of the Sandymount Tower via Bath Avenue to Nelson Pillar

(route 4) followed on 31 August 1932. but the operator continued to construct new trams until 1936. However, on 31 March 1938, the company announced that it was to abandon its tramways over a four-year period. Although initially opposed by the unions, following agreement, the first major conversions occurred on 16 April 1938 with the loss of the Ballybough Parkgate Street and North Quay services (routes 23 and 24). By 31 March 1942, the once large Dublin system had contracted to only three basic routes. These were all suspended in June 1944 as a result of power shortages caused by a drought that had severely limited production of electricity from the hydro-electric plant at Ardnacrusha. At the time, it was suggested that the trams had operated for the last time, but services were reinstated

on 2 October 1944. Thus, when CIÉ took over DUT on 1 January 1945, it inherited three routes operated by some 100 tramcars.

Cork had possessed an early horse tramway but this ceased operation well before the arrival of the trams of the Cork Electric Tramways & Lighting Co. Ltd. The first services operated on 22 December 1898 over the 900mm gauge network. This was just under 2ft 11½in, a gauge selected to permit the (unused) operation of narrow gauge trains from the Cork & Muskerry Light Railway and the Cork, Blackrock & Passage Railway to connect via the tramway track. Eventually, the system comprised just under ten route miles and was operated by a fleet of thirty-five trams, all supplied by Brush between 1898 and 1901.

Four of Cork's 900mm gauge trams – Nos 3 and 15 of 1898, No 24 of 1900 and No 30 of 1901 – are seen in Patrick Street. Also visible is the fleet's works car in the background. *Barry Cross Collection/ Online Transport Archive*

When the first eight Hill of Howth cars were originally delivered, they were painted in a livery of crimson lake and ivory. The higher caging for passengers on the upper deck was a requirement from the Board of Trade designed to protect standing passengers from the proximity of trees and traction columns on the route. *D.W.K. Jones Collection/ Online Transport Archive*

The system was finally to cease operation on 30 September 1931 (an earlier attempt – on 31 March 1931 – had been reversed six days later when the replacement buses proved inadequate), being replaced by the buses of the Irish Omnibus Co., which operated the tramways in the intervening period.

Under the terms of the Great Northern Railway (Ireland) Act of 1897, the railway was empowered to construct a line linking Howth and Sutton stations over the rocky promontory known as the Hill of Howth. These powers were slightly amended in 1900 to permit a deviation and the first section of the 5ft 3in gauge line, from Sutton to Summit, opened on 17 June 1901 with the remainder, from Summit to Howth station, following on 1 August 1901. Initially the service was operated by eight passenger cars; these were supplemented

by an additional two in 1902. Whilst the line was reasonably popular, it was never a financial success – largely as a result of the lack of development of the peninsula – and on six occasions prior to the outbreak of war in 1939 its future was examined in reports. Replacement by bus was considered, but rejected initially as a result of the gradients encountered and later as a result of the GNR(I)'s financial problems, whilst tests to operate the line with a railbus – in 1934 – also came to nothing. As a result, and with the backing of the railway's senior management, the line survived into the post-war era.

A further electric service in the Dublin area was launched on 26 July 1900 when the 5ft 2³⁄₁₆in gauge trams of the Clontarf & Hill of Howth Tramroad Co Ltd opened its line from the existing DUT terminus at Dollymount through to Howth, East Pier.

All twelve of the trams supplied by ERTCW to the Clontarf & Hill of Howth are visible in this posed view. The trams were numbered 301-12 by their new owners. The cars remained open top throughout their life as a result of low railway bridges on the route. All were substantially rebuilt or replaced between 1920 and 1926. *Barry Cross Collection/ Online Transport Archive*

Royal Avenue was Belfast's principal shopping street from the late nineteenth century when it was first constructed. It was used by a number of tram routes heading north out of the city, including that to Cliftonville. Castle Junction, one of the main city termini, was situated at the southern end of the road in the foreground. *Barry Cross Collection/Online Transport Archive*

From opening, the service operated through to Nelson Pillar with crews changing at Dollymount until 1 February 1902. From 1 January 1907 DUT took over sole operation of the line, but the Clontarf & Hill of Howth maintained ownership and its own legal existence until the route was converted to bus operation on 29 March 1941.

Following the conversion of the Dublin & Lucan line, electric services over the line – now renamed the Dublin & Lucan Electric Railway Co – commenced on 8 March 1900. Five new electric cars, Nos 12-16, were acquired from G.F. Milnes & Co whilst three of the steam trailers were regauged and converted to electric traction. Other steam trailers were also regauged and continued in use as trailers post electrification. Under the auspices of the Lucan & Leixlip Electric railway a short – ½-mile – extension was opened in 1910 to Dodsboro. Operation of the Dublin & Lucan ceased at the end of January 1925; the company was

acquired, however, by the Dublin United Tramways Co and, with the line regauged to 5ft 2³⁄₁₆in, services to Chapelizod commenced on 14 May 1928 and thence to Lucan on 27 May 1928. Following objections, the short extension to Dodsboro was not reopened. DUT services to Lucan finally ceased on 14 April 1940.

Following the passage of the Belfast Corporation (Tramways) Act in 1904, the corporation took possession of the horse trams of the Belfast Street Tramways Co on 1 January 1905. Work commenced to convert the routes to electric traction and the first electric trams entered service on 30 November 1905. The entire horse tram network was operated by electric cars by 5 December 1905. The system expanded for the next twenty years; this included the acquisition of the Cavehill & Whitewell line on 2 June 1911 and the final extension – to Ballygomartin – on 23 July 1925. One short section – along Ormeau Road – was abandoned before the First World War but

Dublin & Lucan
No 12; this was one of five cars – Nos 12-16 – supplied by G.F. Milnes & Co in 1900 for the introduction of electric services.
Barry Cross Collection/Online Transport Archive

The Cavehill &
Whitewell Tramway
operated ten
passenger cars;
four, including No
3, are seen in the
depot. *Barry Cross
Collection/Online
Transport Archive*

significant conversion commenced with the abandonment, due to the state of the track, of the outermost section of the Cregagh route in 1936; the same year witnessed the Transport Committee agree to the trial conversion of one route – that along the Falls Road – to trolleybus operation. In 1937, trams were diverted away from the Mountpottinger Road section and, on 28 March 1938, trams ceased to operate on the Falls Road route. On 9 January 1939, it was decided to abandon tram operation over the next five years. Although the war years witnessed a number of tram to trolleybus conversions – Cregagh on 13 February 1941, Castlereagh on 5 June 1941, Stormont on 26 March 1942, Dundonald via Queens Bridge on 16 November 1942 and Dundonald via Albert Bridge on 8 March 1943 – or bus – Ravenhill Road on 5 September 1940 – the war did ensure that the tramways survived longer than originally planned.

The new electric services of the Cavehill & Whitewell Tramway commenced operation on 12 February 1906. In all, ten cars were supplied to the company by Brush but their life with the company was short-lived. On 26 July 1910, Belfast Corporation obtained powers to take over; this was effected on 2 June 1911, when the corporation commenced operation of the route. Eight of the company's fleet passed to the corporation, becoming Nos 193-200. The remaining two were sold to Mansfield & District. Corporation operation of the route continued until replacement by trolleybuses on 23 January 1949.

ISLE OF MAN

As with Guernsey, the Isle of Man is a Crown Dependency and so not covered by the legislative framework established by Westminster. In 1875, an Act was obtained from Tynwald, the Manx parliament, to construct a horse tramway in Douglas. The first section of the 3ft 0in gauge line opened officially on 1 May 1876. This was built and operated by Thomas Lightfoot;

With one of the corporation's cable trams in the foreground, two horse trams – including an open toast-rack – can be seen heading to and from Victoria Pier. *J. Joyce Collection/ Online Transport Archive*

his involvement, however, was short-lived as in 1882 the line was sold to the Isle of Man Tramways Ltd, under whose auspices an extension was opened in 1890 from Burnt Mill Hill to Derby Castle. In 1894, ownership passed to the Isle of Man Tramways & Electric Power Co Ltd, which also owned the MER, but the company went into liquidation in 1900 and, in January 1902, the horse tramway passed to Douglas Corporation. The same year witnessed the line's final extension, to serve Victoria Pier. There were plans – never executed – in the early twentieth century for the line's electrification. From 1927, the horse tramway operated only during the summer months and, in 1935, the last new horse trams were acquired. On 30 September 1939 services ceased at

the end of the summer season; they would not operate again until after the war.

The Isle of Man Tramways & Electric Power Co constructed a second line to serve Douglas; this was the Upper Douglas cable tramway that operated between the Clock Tower and Broadway, both on the Promenade, via Victoria Street and Prospect Hill. Built to the 3ft 0in gauge, the line opened on 15 August 1896. As with the horse tramway, ownership and operation passed to the corporation in 1902. The section between York Road and Broadway was soon closed – the gradient gave rise to safety concerns – but the remainder survived through until abandonment on 19 August 1929, although latterly in the peak summer season only. In all some fifteen cable cars were supplied between

In 1896, G.F. Milnes & Co supplied eight crossbench cars – Nos 71-78 – to the Douglas cable tramway. No 73 illustrated here was one of two to be rescued for preservation in 1976 having spent almost fifty years in use as a bungalow. *Barry Cross Collection/Online Transport Archive*

An early view of G.F. Milnes & Co–built No 9 of 1894 with trailer at Groudle Glen. Note the primitive pantographs at both ends of the power car. *Barry Cross Collection/Online Transport Archive*

I.O.M. GROUDLE TRAM STATION.

E.T.W.D.

1896 and 1911; two – Nos 72 and 73 – were converted into a bungalow after closure. These were rescued in 1976 and, using the parts from the two cars, one cable car was created.

In 1892, the Douglas Bay Estate Ltd obtained powers to construct a 3ft 0in line from Douglas to Groudle Glen at a time when speculators were seeking to develop the northern part of the island. The company was taken over by the Douglas & Laxey Bay Electric Tramway Co Ltd (incorporated on 3 May 1893) before the line opened on 7 September 1893. The new owner obtained powers to double the line and extend it to Laxey; work started in February 1894 and the Laxey extension opened on 23 July 1894. By this date the company name had changed to the Isle of Man Tramways & Electric Power Co Ltd; this company, the creation of Alexander Bruce, eventually owned the MER as well as both the horse and cable tramways in Douglas and the Snaefell Mountain

Railway. In 1897, powers were obtained to extend the MER to Ramsey; the first section, to Ballure (where a temporary depot was sited), opened on 5 August 1898 with the line to Ramsey being completed throughout on 24 July 1899. On 18 August 1902, following the collapse of Dumbell's Bank (in which Bruce was also involved) the previous February, the MER and Snaefell passed to the Manx Electric Railway Co Ltd. The line carried both passenger and freight traffic, the latter included livestock, stone and general merchandise, but its financial position deteriorated from the early 1930s and its survival through to the war was aided by the willingness of the debenture holders to forego payment.

Owned by the New General Traction Co, the Douglas Southern Electric Tramway (later the Douglas Head Marine Drive) was the only line – railway or tramway – built on the island to standard gauge. The 4½-mile long line extended southwards

The Douglas
Head Marine Drive employed eight open-top trams, such as No 4 shown here. Similar tram No 1 now forms part of the NTM collection.
Barry Cross Collection/Online Transport Archive

from Douglas to Port Soderick, providing passengers with spectacular views of the Irish Sea and the cliffs. The line opened on 2 September 1896 and operated through until 15 September 1939 when services were suspended for the war. The service was operated by eight four-wheel open-top cars with matching trailers. Operation was never resumed with Marine Drive being taken over by the corporation and rebuilt as a road in 1946. When the tram fleet was disposed of after the war, No 1 was secured for preservation and is now housed at the NTM.

The first proposals to construct a line up the 2,200ft-high Snaefell were made in 1887/88 by George Nobel Fell, the son of John Barraclough Fell who had developed the 'Fell' system of rack railway, the first such system in the world. This scheme did not proceed but a second plan in 1895 was more successful. Not requiring an Act of Tynwald – it operated over privately-owned land or land that was easily acquired – construction of the 3ft 6in gauge line began under the auspices of the Snaefell Mountain Railway Association. Services were first operated on 21 August 1895 but, in December 1895, ownership passed to the Isle of Man Tramways & Electric Power Co Ltd, which also owned the MER. This company collapsed seven years later and its assets passed to the new Manx Electric Railway Co.

WALES

The development of tramways was governed in Wales by the provisions of the 1870 Tramways Act although the oldest horse-operated line predated the act; indeed, with its origins in the Oystermouth Railway, the Swansea & Mumbles could claim to be the oldest passenger railway in the world.

The Oystermouth Railway was initially constructed under an Act of Parliament in 1804 and the line opened to carry freight traffic two years later. Following approval, passenger services commenced on 25 March 1807, making the line the first to transport passengers in the world. However, operation of the line ceased

in 1826 and it was not until the 1860s – following the line's conversion from 4ft 0in to 4ft 8½in and relaying – that horse-drawn passenger services recommenced. However, from 1874, a legal quirk meant that the Swansea Improvements & Tramways Co was able to operate horse trams in competition on the Oystermouth line; as a result, the latter responded three years later by introducing steam-operated services over the line. The competition – which was not always gentlemanly – was to continue through to 1896 when the Swansea Improvements & Tramways Co withdrew its horse trams.

There were two horse tramways that served Cardiff. The first of these was the Cardiff Tramways Co Ltd which introduced the first of its standard gauge trams on 12 July 1872. The network eventually extended to about 6¼ route miles, operated at its peak by 52 trams. The second operator was the Cardiff District & Penarth Tramway Co Ltd; this company opened its 2½-mile standard gauge route from Adamsdown to Grangetown on 28 November 1881. The line was leased to Solomon Andrews, whose horse buses operated in competition with the horse trams of the Cardiff Tramways Co. In 1888, operation of the later tramway passed to Provincial, which also operated the lines of the Cardiff Tramways Co. The corporation took over operation of the Cardiff Tramways Co on 1 January 1902; the last horse tram operated on these routes on 17 October 1902 as part of the process of electrification. The smaller company survived until the corporation took over in 1903; the last horse trams operated over the route on 10 February 1903. One Cardiff horse tram survives in preservation.

The 2ft 4½in gauge Glyn Valley Tramway operated westwards from Chirk through the valley to Glyn Ceiriog. Passenger services ran over some 8¼ miles with a number of freight branches linking the main line with the numerous quarries along the valley. The line was authorised by an Act of 10 August

A horse-drawn passenger service on the Oystermouth Railway in a view that dates to shortly after the reintroduction of passenger services in 1860. *Barry Cross Collection/Online Transport Archive*

No 24 was one of the fleet of standard gauge horse trams operated by the Cardiff Tramways Co Ltd; sister car No 21 was restored after being rescued for preservation. *Barry Cross Collection/Online Transport Archive*

1870, following the failure of an earlier proposal to build a standard gauge line, with construction commencing in June 1872. The line opened to freight traffic in April 1873 and horse-operated passenger services commenced on 1 April 1874. Horse and gravity were used exclusively until 1885 when steam power was authorised; it was not until 1891, however, that steam replaced horse traction on passenger services.

The Neath & District Tramways Co Ltd commenced operation of a standard gauge horse tramway from Briton Ferry to Skewen on 19 November 1875. The single route, which was just under four route miles in length, passed to Neath Corporation along with eight trams on 7 August 1896. The corporation then leased the operation of the line to the British Gas Traction Co Ltd and, following the introduction of gas-powered trams, the last horse cars operated in 1899.

On 1 February 1875, the Newport (Mon) Tramways Co Ltd opened a short route – just over a mile in length – from the town centre to the docks. The company continued to operate the line until 28 July 1894, when, following purchase by the corporation and extension by three miles, Solomon Andrews continued to operate the route under licence from 30 July 1894 until 29 July 1901 when the corporation took over. Following electrification, the last horse trams operated on 3 November 1903.

The Swansea Improvements & Tramways Co Ltd opened the first sections of its standard gauge horse tramway, from College Street to Morriston and to St Helens on 12 April 1878. Eventually the horse network extended over some 5½ route miles and a total of twenty-five cars were employed. The last horse trams operated in 1901 and were replaced by company-owned electric trams.

On 1 November 1876, the Wrexham District Tramways Co commenced operation over a single 3ft 6in gauge route, just over 3¼ miles in length, from the town southwards to Johnstown. In all, three trams were owned and operation ceased on 26 April 1901, some two years before electric trams arrived.

In 1892 the Newport (Mon) Tramways Co replaced its original fleet of five single-deck cars with eight open-top double-deck examples. One of these is seen on High Street. *Barry Cross Collection/ Online Transport Archive*

High Street and Corn Exchange, Newport (Mon)

In all, the Swansea Improvements & Tramways Co Ltd operated twenty-five horse trams; No 16 is seen in 1890. *Barry Cross Collection/ Online Transport Archive*

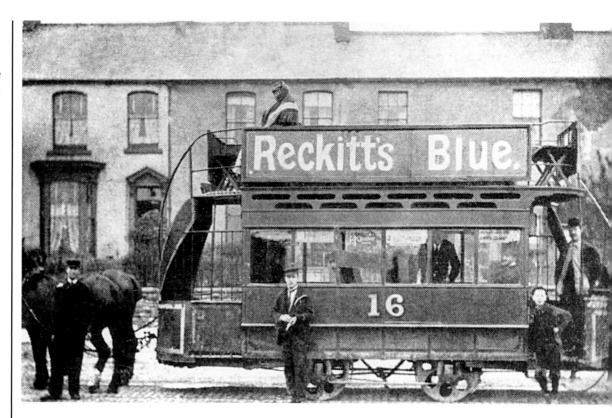

The Wrexham District Tramways Co operated three horse trams; No 2 was an open-top car supplied by Starbuck. *Barry Cross Collection/ Online Transport Archive*

The Harlech Tramway, which ran some 600 yards from the Cambrian Railways line to the beach, is believed to have been 2ft 0in gauge. Promoted by Godfrey Morton, the line, which is recorded on a contemporary large-scale Ordnance Survey map although other details are sketchy, opened in July 1878 and operated until about 1886.

The first horse trams to serve Llanelli were the 3ft 0in gauge trams of the Llanelly Tramways Co Ltd. These operated over a one-mile route that linked the town centre to the railway station. Services commenced on 28 September 1882 and the company employed five trams. In 1900, the company was taken over by the Llanelly & District Electric Lighting & Traction Co Ltd in 1900. The original horse tramway ceased operation on 31 March 1908 when it was closed for reconstruction to standard gauge; this was completed and services were reintroduced, using three ex-London double-deck horse cars, over a slightly longer route. Horse trams survived until replacement by electric cars on 19 July 1911.

Promoted by the Pontypridd & Rhondda Valley Tramway Co, a 3ft 6in gauge horse tramway extending for three route miles between Pontypridd and Porth commenced operation in March 1888. Operated by Solomon Andrews & Sons, the route was the only part of a longer — 12¼ — route mile network originally authorised. The operation was acquired by BET in 1899 and, the following year, the new operator sought powers to electrify the route but these were objected to by Pontypridd and Rhondda councils. In 1904, following an epidemic two years earlier that had severely reduced the number of horses available (and thus the service operated), the two councils acquired the tramway with the route being split at Trehafod. Horse operation had effectively ceased in July the previous year.

Pwllheli developed as a holiday resort in the late nineteenth century. The town was served by two small horse tramways, neither of which were to be converted to electric traction. The older of the two was the 3ft 0in gauge Pwllheli & Llanbedrog

The Llanelly Tramways Co Ltd operated five single-deck horse trams between 1882 and 1908. *Barry Cross Collection/Online Transport Archive*

One of the Pwllheli & Llanbedrog Tramway's fleet of open horse trams stands at the town terminus; in all, the operator possessed some twenty trams during its thirty-one-year existence. *Barry Cross Collection/Online Transport Archive*

Pwllheli UDC owned one fully-enclosed car, which was supplied by the Midland Railway Carriage & Wagon Co Ltd; this tram's body was eventually secured for preservation and restored. *Barry Cross Collection/Online Transport Archive*

Tramway operated by S. Andrews & Sons Ltd. Originally a mineral line opened in 1894, this was adapted for passenger operation between Pwllheli station and Llanbedrog – a distance of almost four miles. Services commenced on 1 August 1896. A varied fleet was operated, including the three cars that once operated the corporation route. These were acquired in 1921. Services last operated on 28 October 1927; that night, part of the route was damaged by a storm and the decision was taken not to reopen. The second line was operated by Pwllheli Corporation and extended for about half-a-mile from the station to the beach. The 2ft 6in line, which was operated by three trams (two open and one enclosed), opened on 24 July 1899 and was to close at the end of the summer season in 1920 (probably during September).

One of two lines situated south of Barmouth, the 2ft 0in Fairbourne Tramway was constructed to provide a link between Penrhyn Point Ferry and Fairbourne. The two-mile line originally opened in 1895 but, following a transfer of ownership in 1911, the track was converted to 15in gauge in 1916 and steam operation replaced horse power.

The Barmouth Junction & Arthog Tramway was a two-mile 3ft 0in gauge line that was built to link Mawddach Crescent with Barmouth Junction – later Morfa Mawddach – station. It was promoted by Andrew Solomons as part of his plans to develop Arthog as a holiday resort. The line opened in August 1899 but was to last only until to August 1903; after services ceased, the line's one car was transferred to the Pwllheli & Llanbedrog service.

In order to counter the competition from the horse-powered vehicles operated by the Swansea Improvements & Tramways Co, the Oystermouth Railway introduced steam traction on 17 August 1877. The Oystermouth was officially renamed the Swansea & Mumbles Railway on 26 July 1893. The same year saw the line extended to Southend and, five years later, the final extension to Mumbles Pier followed on 10 May 1898. Following an Act of 9 August 1899, the line was leased to the Swansea Improvements & Tramways Co, which was, by this time, under the control of BET. Although there were plans early in the twentieth century to electrify the line – two experimental accumulator cars

Although better known today as a miniature railway, the Fairbourne Railway started life as a 2ft 0in gauge horse tramway. *J. Joyce Collection/ Online Transport Archive*

A well-laden steam-hauled passenger service on the Oystermouth Railway. *Barry Cross Collection/Online Transport Archive*

In 1902 the Swansea & Mumbles acquired two double-deck accumulator trams; never successful, they were converted into conventional trailers for steam operation the following year. *Barry Cross Collection/Online Transport Archive*

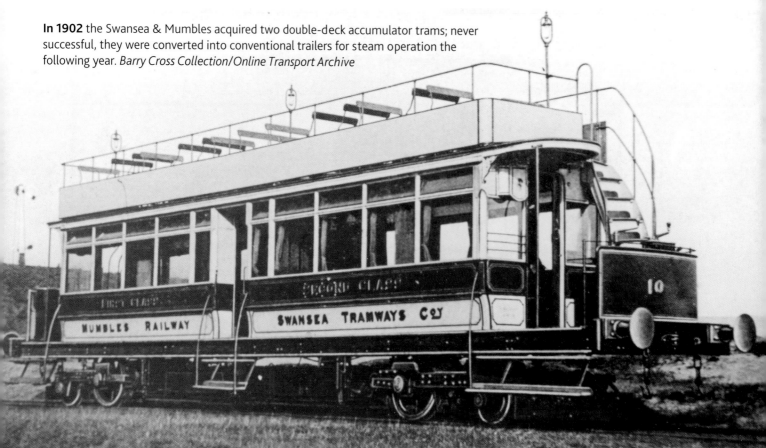

were acquired in October 1902 rather than undertake the physical electrification of the route but these proved unsuccessful and were converted to conventional steam-hauled trailers the following year – it was not until 1929 that the last steam passenger services operated.

Although the Swansea Improvements & Tramways Co Ltd was primarily an operator of horse trams in the pre-electric age, for a brief two-year period – between 1882 and 1884 – the company employed two Hughes-built steam engines on the route to Cwmbwrla from the line's opening.

Following authorisation to convert the Glyn Valley Tramway to steam operation, locomotives were borrowed from the Snailbeach District Railways to permit the line's reconstruction and the diversion at the eastern end to serve Chirk station, on the Shrewsbury-Wrexham line. New steam-hauled freight services were introduced in 1888 with passenger services commencing in 1891. The line's financial position deteriorated after the First World War and it deteriorated further in 1932, when a competing bus service was introduced. Passenger services ceased on 6 April 1933 and freight on 6 July 1935, after which the line was closed and dismantled the following year.

Apart from horse and steam trams, Swansea could also claim a short cable tramway. This was the 3ft 6in gauge line of the Swansea Constitution Hill Incline Tramway Co Ltd, which commenced operation on 27 August 1898 over a route that extended for less than a quarter of a mile from St George Street to Hannover Street with an average gradient of 1 in 5. Two Brush-built cars were operated over the line but it was never a financial success and, in the local *Evening Express* a notice appeared on 3 October 1901 intimating that the line's future was in doubt and that it had been offered to the local corporation. This offer was declined and the last services operated on 5 October 1901.

Although looking like a cable line, the Great Orme tramway is effectively two long funiculars, where the two cars on

Glyn Valley No 2 *Sir Theodore* was one of two 0-4-2Ts supplied by Beyer Peacock in 1888 to permit steam operation of the line. It was one of four locomotives owned by the tramway during its history; all were scrapped in 1936. *Barry Cross Collection/Online Transport Archive*

Glyn Valley Train   Photo by Burr

The two Brush-built cars of the short-lived Swansea Constitution Hill Incline Tramway Co Ltd pass; the overhead was used for signalling purposes. *Barry Cross Collection/Online Transport Archive*

On 23 August 1932, the Great Orme Tramway suffered its only fatal accident when No 4 ran away on the lower section, killing its driver and a 12-year-old passenger. The subsequent Inspector's report was highly critical of the tramway. With the tramway's lack of adequate insurance cover to cover the claims led to the Sheriff taking possession of the line on 7 June 1933 and the Board agreeing to seek a winding-up order the same day. Although the order was granted on 24 July 1933, a creditors' meeting on 24 August 1933 agreed that improvements should be made to the braking system and that every effort should be made to sell the tramway as a going concern. *D.W. K. Jones Collection/Online Transport Archive*

each section are permanently connected to the cable and pass at the predetermined passing loops. Construction of the line was authorised by the Great Orme Tramways Act of 1898 and, following fund raising and land acquisition, construction of the 3ft 6in gauge line commenced in October 1900. Public service on the lower section commenced on 31 July 1902 and on the upper section on 8 July 1903; the lower section is 872yd in length and the upper 827yd with average gradients of 1 in 6½ and 1 in 15½ respectively. To operate the service, four bogie cars – two for each section – were acquired from Hurst Nelson; a small number of freight vehicles were also owned but this traffic ceased by 1911. For thirty years the line operated without incident; however an accident on the lower section involving No 4 on 23 August 1932 resulted in two fatalities and the suspension of services; a highly critical inspector's report was issued the following year. For a period, it looked as though the line's future was in doubt as the company lacked adequate insurance cover and, following the sheriff taking possession of the line on 7 July 1933, the board decided the same day to seek a winding up order. This was granted on 24 July 1933; however, a meeting of creditors held on 25 August 1933, resulted in a decision being made to provide improved braking and to try and sell the business as a going concern. The tramway thus reopened on 17 May 1934 and was sold to a new consortium in December that year. The new owners created the Great Orme Railway Ltd in March 1935 and it was in this guise that the tramway entered into the post-war era.

For the last four years of their operation, the gas trams of Neath were operated by the corporation; this view, therefore, of No 19 – one of the trams transferred from Lytham – must date to between 1916 and 1920. *Barry Cross Collection/ Online Transport Archive*

In 1897 Neath Corporation acquired the horse tramways operated by the Neath & District Tramways Co; however, instead of the authorised electrification, the operation of the line was leased to the British Gas Traction Co Ltd (the Provincial Gas Traction Co Ltd from 1902). Gas operation of the four-mile standard gauge line commenced on 31 August 1899. Four cars

Swansea No 35 was new in 1933 – one of the last trams delivered to the operator – and was built in the company's own works on a home-produced four-wheel truck. *Barry Cross Collection/Online Transport Archive*

were supplied new and the fleet was supplemented by cars transferred from the company's operation at Lytham St Annes. Neath Corporation took over operation in 1916 and the gas trams operated for the last time on 8 August 1920, when they were replaced by the buses of the South Wales Transport Co Ltd. One of the gas cars, No 1, was rescued for preservation in the 1980s and has been subsequently restored.

The earliest electric trams to operate in Wales were those of the Swansea Improvements & Tramways Co Ltd, whose services commenced on 30 June 1900. The original horse routes were all converted and, with extensions, the standard gauge network eventually extended over almost 13½ route miles with a maximum fleet of seventy-nine trams. As late as 1933, the company was still constructing replacement cars but that year also witnessed the first conversion to bus operation with the demise of the section from Morriston to Ynysforgan and the final trams operated on 29 June 1937. The trams were all replaced by buses operated by South Wales Transport, another subsidiary of BET.

In Merthyr Tydfil, a further BET subsidiary – the Merthyr Tydfil Electric Traction & Lighting Co Ltd – commenced operation over a 3ft 6in gauge electric tramway on 6 April 1901. Two routes were operated, from Graham Street to Bush Inn with a branch to Cefn Bridge; following an extension to the latter in 1914, the total route mileage came to 3½. Although the last 'new' trams – acquired second-hand from Birmingham – were acquired in 1933, the council acquired the tramway in 1939 with the intention of converting it to bus operation. The last trams operated on 23 August 1939.

Cardiff Corporation took over operation of the company-operated routes in January 1902 with the exception of that built by the Cardiff District & Penarth Harbour Tramway Co Ltd, which passed to corporation ownership the following year. Work progressed quickly in the system's electrification, with the first

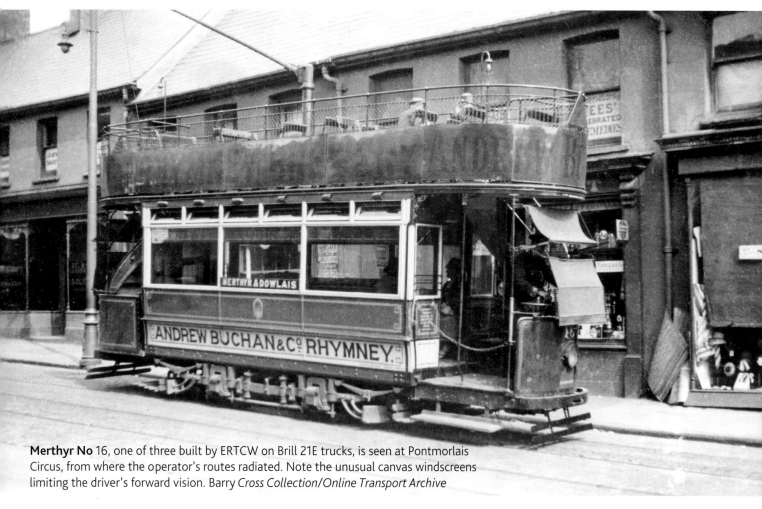

Merthyr No 16, one of three built by ERTCW on Brill 21E trucks, is seen at Pontmorlais Circus, from where the operator's routes radiated. Note the unusual canvas windscreens limiting the driver's forward vision. Barry *Cross Collection/Online Transport Archive*

Cardiff's first electric trams, such as No 5 seen here in Queen Street, were supplied by ERTCW on Brill 21E trucks in 1902. *Barry Cross Collection/Online Transport Archive*

electric cars – on the Canton and Cathedral Road routes – commencing operation on 2 May 1902. The early years witnessed expansion but, from 1905 through to the appointment of R. J. Horsfield as general manager in 1920, there was little development. The new decade, however, saw considerable fleet modernisation and a number of extensions, the last of which saw the Cathedral Road route extended on 6 August 1928. This saw the system at its peak with 19½ route miles operated by 142 trams. Horsfield departed to take over at Leeds the following month and, thereafter, the tram in Cardiff was under threat.

The new manager – William Forbes from Aberdeen – was perceived to be more pro-bus. On 4 April 1930, the Salisbury Road route – one of a number in the city historically affected by low railway bridges – was abandoned. The threat to the trams was further increased in 1934 when the Cardiff Corporation Act gave powers to operate trolleybuses in the city, although it was not until May 1939 that approval was given to introduce them and the first services were not operated until 1942. The poor condition of track on the Splott and Grangetown routes resulted in their conversion on 11 October 1936, although the track in Adamsdown was retained for diversionary use. By the outbreak of war, the Cardiff network comprised routes to Canton, Gabalfa, Roath Park, Pengam, Pier Head, Cathedral Road (Llandaff Fields) and Clarence Road. The last-named route was, however, to see the introduction of the first five trolleybuses to serve Cardiff on 1 March 1942. As more trolleybuses were delivered, so the trams were eliminated from the Cathedral Road route on 8 November 1942 with trolleybuses now operating from Clarence Road to Cathedral Road via Wood Street.

Following the closure of the horse tramway in Wrexham in 1903, a BET subsidiary, the Wrexham & District Electric Tramways Ltd, converted the line to electric traction and extended it. Electric services over the 4½-mile 3ft 6in gauge line commenced on 4 April 1903. Although an extension southwards to Ruabon was authorised, this was never built and all services ceased on 31 March 1927, being replaced by buses. A fleet of ten open-top trams supplied by Brush operated the line for its entire history.

Following its acquisition of the town's horse tramways Newport Corporation undertook the conversion of the bulk of the system to electric traction and the first new electric trams operated on 9 April 1903. Further extensions saw the network eventually reach just over 8½ route miles. In all, some fifty-five trams were operated by the corporation, the last new cars being delivered in 1922. However, two routes were converted to bus operation in 1928 and 1930; the remaining routes survived until 1937 with the last trams operating on 5 September 1937.

Following its acquisition of its section of the Pontypridd & Rhondda Valley Tramway Co in 1904, Pontypridd UDC electrified its section to Trehafod, in 1907, having initially constructed a new route between Treforest and Cilfynydd, on which services had commenced on 5 March 1905. Initially, the two sections were separate but were eventually to be connected. From July 1919, through services were operated through Trehafod to Rhondda and beyond; these continued until December 1927. The Trehafod service was abandoned early in 1931 with the remaining trams being converted to trolleybus operation on 30 August 1931. In all, the UDC operated some thirty-one trams, the last five of which were delivered in 1920, over a five-mile route network.

The late nineteenth century witnessed a boom in the future North Wales holiday resorts and, on 2 June 1899, the Llandudno & Colwyn Bay Light Railway Order was made but little subsequent progress followed. The original order was amended by the Llandudno & Colwyn Bay Light Railway (Deviation) Order of 26 September 1903 and contracts for construction were let in 1904.

Wrexham No 7 was one of the fleet's ten passenger cars; all were supplied by Brush on Brush A trucks in 1903. *Barry Cross Collection/ Online Transport Archive*

Newport No 44 was one of three cars built by UEC on Brill 21E trucks in 1909. *Barry Cross Collection/Online Transport Archive*

One of six open-top trams (Nos 7-12) supplied to Pontypridd UDC by Brush on Brill 22E bogies in 1904, No 9 (along with the remainder) received lengthened canopies in 1914 and short top-deck covers between 1921 and 1923. *Barry Cross Collection/Online Transport Archive*

Again, however, some progress was made despite the company, and its immediate successor, both failing before the creation of a third company – the Llandudno & District Tramway Construction Co Ltd – in July 1907. Limited public services over the 3ft 6in gauge line commenced on 19 October 1907 although the full service did not commence until the following month. The initial route was extended from Rhos to Station Road in Colwyn Bay on 7 June 1908 and, on 21 April 1909, the operator was renamed the Llandudno & Colwyn Bay Electric Railway Ltd. The final extension from Station Road to the Queens Hotel in Old Colwyn opened on 26 March 1915.

In 1917, the first contraction of the line occurred with the closure of the short section of line to West Shore in Llandudno. Also during the First World War permission was granted, for the first time, by the Board of Trade to operate double-deck trams, although it would not be until the mid-1930s that the company exercised

these powers. During the interwar years, the company undertook considerable work on the tramway, including much doubling of the route, although the 1915 extension remained largely single track. With the arrival of increased bus operation in the late 1920s, this section was to become vulnerable and, in 1929, it was decided to close the extension. The last trams operated beyond Colwyn Bay to Old Colwyn on 21 September 1930. The 1930s witnessed considerable replacement of the fleet with second-hand cars being acquired from Accrington and Bournemouth. The line was thus one of three electric tramways in Wales to survive through to the Second World War and beyond.

In 1900, the existing horse tram operator in Llanelli was purchased by the Llanelly & District Electric Lighting & Traction Co Ltd. The new operator converted the line to standard gauge, operating it by second-hand ex-London horse cars before electric services were introduced on 19 July 1911.

In 1907 the Midland Railway Carriage & Wagon Co Ltd supplied 14 single-deck trams for the opening of the Llandudno & Colwyn Bay line; No 9 is seen on Gloddaeth Street in a postcard franked 30 May 1908. *Barry Cross Collection/ Online Transport Archive*

In all about 6¼ route miles were operated with sixteen trams owned. The last new trams were acquired in 1920; in addition, two second-hand cars were acquired from Mansfield & District in 1918 but these were never operated and returned to Nottinghamshire two years later. The company became the Llanelly & District Electric Supply Co Ltd in 1924 and the final trams operated on 16 February 1933, being replaced by company-owned trolleybuses.

Rhondda UDC acquired its section of the erstwhile Pontypridd & Rhondda Valley Tramway Co in 1904 and then leased the line to the National Electric Construction Co Ltd; this company established the Rhondda Tramways Co Ltd in 1906 and work was undertaken both to electrify the original route and to extend the line. Electric services were initially introduced on 11 July 1908 and, following extensions, the network eventually extended to just under thirty route miles and was operated by a fleet of fifty-four trams. Services ceased on 1 February 1934, being replaced by buses.

In 1911, Aberdare UDC obtained powers to construct a 3ft 6in gauge line from Trecynon to Aberaman. This was opened on 9 October 1913. Although the UDC had powers to extend the line, these were not pursued, with trolleybuses being introduced in January 1914. In all, the UDC operated twenty-six trams, the last new cars being acquired in 1921. Tramway operation ceased on 31 March 1935 with the trams being replaced by council-owned buses.

The last new first-generation tramway to commence operation in the British Isles was, ironically, the world's oldest passenger carrying line — the Swansea & Mumbles. In 1899, the Swansea Improvements & Tramways Co Ltd took on a 999-year on the line; the new operator continued to operate steam-hauled services, using large double-deck trailers for passenger accommodation. In 1927, the lease was again transferred to a new operator — the South Wales Transport Co Ltd — which commenced the electrification of the line. New electric services, using 13 Brush-built double-deck trams, were introduced on 2 March 1929.

Two of Llanelly & District's fleet of 16 trams stand in the operator's depot. No 13 was one of four cars supplied by UEC in 1912 whilst No 15 was one of two — the last new cars supplied to the undertaking — built by English Electric in 1920. Both were fitted with Peckham P22 trucks. *Barry Cross Collection/Online Transport Archive*

Rhondda No 34 stands in Partridge Road, Trealaw; this was one of fifty trams supplied by Brush on Brush AA trucks for the opening of the system in 1908. *Barry Cross Collection/Online Transport Archive*

In all, Aberdare UDC operated twenty-six electric trams; Nos 11-20 were single-deck cars built by Brush on Peckham P22 trucks that were new in 1913. *Barry Cross Collection/Online Transport Archive*

The Pier, Mumbles

With the 1898-built pier in the background, one of the then new Brush-built electric trams stands at the western terminus of the Swansea & Mumbles line. *Barry Cross Collection/Online Transport Archive*

BELFAST

GLENGORMLEY

GREENCASTLE

BELFAST

LIGONIEL

CLIFTONVILLE
&
OLDPARK

NCR
STATION

QUEEN'S
ROAD

BALLYGOMARTIN

QUEEN'S QUAY
STATION

STORMONT

SPRINGFIELD

DUNDONALD

DONEGALL
ROAD

CASTLEREAGH

FALLS ROAD

CREGAGH

STRANMILLS

ORMEAU
ROAD

BALMORAL

MALONE ROAD

The last new trams delivered to Belfast were the 50 'McCreary' cars delivered during 1935 and 1936. Construction was split between English Electric and the locally-based Service Motor Works. The first to be constructed by the latter, No 393, is pictured at Ligoniel; the Ligoniel route was destined to be one of the last to survive, with all day services not being withdrawn until October 1953. *R. W. A. Jones/Online Transport Archive*

One of the more unusual aspects of the Belfast system was the two sidings located within the railway stations at York Road and Queen's Quay; seen here entering the latter is 'McCreary' No 428. *R.W.A. Jones/Online Transport Archive*

'Moffett' No 328 is seen on 8 June 1948 near to the depot at Ardoyne; this was one of two depots that were to survive through to the system's closure in 1954. In the distance, a 'McCreary' car can be seen outbound on a route 25 service. *John Meredith/Online Transport Archive*

The only conversions of 1949 occurred on 23 January 1949 when the services to Glengormley were replaced by trolleybuses. On 5 June 1948, No 268 is seen at the terminus. Note the unusual upper-deck window arrangements. *John Meredith/Online Transport Archive*

On 12 January 1950, No 299 stands at Greencastle; this service was converted to trolleybus operation on 21 August 1950. Evidence of the replacement is clear with the newly-erected trolleybus overhead. *John Meredith/Online Transport Archive*

Ballygomartin was one of three routes converted to bus operation in November 1952; here 'Moffett' No 327 stands at the terminus displaying the post-1951 route number. *R.W.A Jones/ Online Transport Archive*

The service along Queen's Road was to survive until the end of the system; it was used heavily by workers to and from the shipyards. In peak hours, lines of extra trams were provided. Here a number of trams – including 'McCreary' No 437 and 'Chamberlain' No 357 (later preserved) – await their next duties. *R.W.A. Jones/Online Transport Archive*

Belfast Corporation entered the war with the avowed intention of seeing the tram system converted by 1944; despite a number of conversions, this expectation had proved impossible to achieve (partly as a result of wartime deliveries of new trolleybuses being only 88 of the 112 ordered, plus problems in obtaining other necessary equipment). At the start of 1945, the network of tram services was still significant, although most of the routes in the east of the city had been converted.

The first significant event in 1945 was the 'suspension' of the route 16 – the service to Ormeau Road via Botanic Avenue. The withdrawal – announced as a temporary measure in the local press – was as the result of the need to replace a sewer in Botanic Avenue. The 16 was diverted to operate via Cromac Street (which was the route of the existing 15 service to Ormeau Road). In reality, services were never restored to the Botanic Avenue section as, when the sewer work was completed six months later, it was decided not to relay the tram track.

With peace restored, the corporation returned to tramway conversion. The first route to be converted was on 5 May 1946, when route 20 (City Hall to Bloomfield) – the last in the east of the city – was replaced by trolleybuses. This conversion permitted the closure of the Knock depot, situated on the closed route to Dundonald.

There were to be two conversions the following year; on 20 April 1947, routes 37/38, to Donegall Road, were operated by trams for the last time and, on 31 August 1947, route 14 (Castle Junction to Cliftonville) was replaced by buses. The next conversions were the two routes to Ormeau Road – the 15 and 16 – which both now ran out of the city via Cromac Street; these were converted to trolleybus operation on 19 April 1948. This was the only conversion during 1948 and, despite the significant reduction in the size of the system, the trams in Belfast still carried almost as many passengers in 1948 (122 million) as the buses and trolleybuses combined (135 million).

The next casualty, on 23 January 1949, saw the conversion of routes 3 and 5 from Castle Junction to Glengormley to trolleybus operation; these – at 5½ miles in length – represented the corporation's longest tram routes; this service had been inherited from the Cavehill & Whitewell Tramway Co. The period also witnessed the end of the surviving ex-horse cars; four – Nos 213/44/49/50 – had been retained as works cars but were to be withdrawn during 1949. No 249 was retained for preservation. Concurrent with the conversion of the Glengormley route was the closure of the Salisbury Avenue depot to trams.

There was now an eighteen-month gap until the next abandonment; this occurred on 21 August 1950 and saw the conversion of the section of route 29 that served the LMS station via Corporation Street replaced by buses. The Stranmillis route, which had previously been linked with the LMS Station, was diverted to run to Queens Road via the High Street instead of along Chichester Street. This conversion was followed on 2 October 1950 when route 7 – from City Hall to Greencastle – was converted to trolleybus operation. This was not quite the end of trams along York Road; until 3 July 1953, they operated in peak hours from Fortwilliam Shore Road – a short working of the longer route – to Queen's Road for the conveyance of workers to and from Harland and Woolf shipyards. The Greencastle conversion was the last to trolleybus; thereafter diesel buses were preferred and the life of the remaining tram routes was prolonged as a result of delays in obtaining buses for the replacement services.

On 4 February 1951, in order to avoid confusion, all route numbers were rationalised; trolleybus services were numbered between 1 and 39, tram between 50 and 69 and bus between 70 and 99. The first service to be abandoned in 1951 was that to Oldpark Road, which was converted to bus operation on 29 April. This was followed on 29 July when trams last operated over the route to Stranmillis; this service had been linked with the service to Queen's Road; the latter now operated through to Springfield Road. The final conversion of 1951 was the Malone Road route, which last operated on 4 November. The 1951 conversions permitted the closure of Shore Road depot.

It was to be a year before the next conversions, but 9 November 1952 was to see three routes – Balmoral, Ballygomartin and Springfield – all operate for the last time. In May 1952, such was the demand for capacity during the Balmoral Show, that sixteen stored 'DK1' trams were temporarily restored to service. Again, the three services were all replaced by bus. From 15 March 1953, the corporation's main workshops at Sandy Row were closed to the trams; the system was definitely entering its final phase.

In early 1953 the problems in obtaining replacement buses was solved by the arrival of the first of 100 ex-London Transport buses; these started to appear on the Crumlin Road routes on 9 February 1953 but the trams continued to predominate for a period. By this date, the Belfast system had contracted effectively to the two routes to Ligoniel – via the Shankhill Road or the Crumlin Road – and Queen's Road plus surviving peak hour only services to Fortwilliam Shore Road, to Windsor Park and to Mackie's Foundry on the York Road, Lisburn Road and Springfield Road respectively; all of these peak hour services operated for the last time on 3 July 1953 as more buses became available.

All-day service on the Belfast system came to an end on 10/11 October 1953 when trams were withdrawn from the two routes to Ligoniel as well as that along Queen's Road; thereafter the only tram operation in the city was during peak hours and even this gradually diminished as an increasing number of replacement buses became available.

On 30 October 1953, trams made use of the siding at Queen's Quay station, off the Queen's Road route, for the last time; this facility and that at York Road station were unique in the British Isles in providing an undercover connection between tram and train services; their loss was much mourned by the passengers who faced a walk in the rain to pick up the replacement buses. The peak hour only services to Ligoniel and Queen's Road ceased effectively on 10 February 1954 but it was not until 28 February that the official closure took place when a procession of twelve 'Chamberlain' cars made their farewell journey from Queen's Road to the depot at Ardoyne; the official last car was No 389.

Following closure of the system, the fleet was gradually transferred from Ardoyne depot to Mountpottinger depot for scrapping; the last car made its way for the final time on 17 June 1954. In all, two electric cars – ex-horse car No 249 and 'Chamberlain' No 357 – survived into preservation.

DEPOTS

There were seven depots that served the Belfast system during the electric era, all bar one of which survived into the post-war years. The one exception was Falls Road, which had closed in 1938. The main workshops were situated at Sandy Row; these were to close to the trams in 1953. Knock depot closed in 1946, Salisbury Avenue in 1949 and Shore Road in 1951; this left two depots – Ardoyne and Mountpottinger – still operational in 1954 when the system closed. Of the seven, all bar Ardoyne and Shore Road had been inherited from the horse trams. Shore Road was built in 1904 whilst Ardoyne was built originally in 1912 and extended the following year to house trams required for the route extensions opened that year.

CLOSURES

5 January 1945	16 – Ormeau Road (via Botanic Avenue; service initially suspended due to sewer work then completely abandoned)
5 May 1946	20 – City Hall to Bloomfield
20 April 1947	37/38 – Donegall Road

31 August 1947	14 – Cliftonville		(Lisburn Road)/ Queen's Road to
19 April 1948	15/16 – Ormeau Road (via Cromac Street)		Mackie's Foundry (Springfield Road)/ Queen's Road to
23 January 1949	3/5 – Castle Junction to Glengormley		Fitzwilliam Shore Road
21 August 1950	29 – LMS station (via Corporation Street)	10/11 October 1953	All-day services on the remaining
2 October 1950	7 – City Hall to Greencastle		services to Ligoniel (via Crumlin Road
29 April 1951	City to Oldpark Road		and via Shankill Road) and Queen's
29 July 1951	Stranmillis		Road
13 June 1951	York Road station bay	30 October 1953	Queen's Quay station
4 November 1951	Malone Road		
9 November 1952	Balmoral/ Ballygomartin/ Springfield	28 February 1954	Official last tram
3 July 1953	Withdrawal of limited peak hour services from Queen's Road to Windsor Park		

2-5, 10/12-14/16-18, 23/26/27/29, 30/32/33/36/37, 40/42/43/46/48-51/54/55/57/58, 61-65, 73, 80/88/89, 94/95/98, 100-05/07/08/10/ 11/13/14/ 16/18/19/22/24/26/28//30/32/34/37/40/41/44/46/ 47/49/51/53/55/58/62/63/66-70

Belfast Standard
No 153 in the original red and cream livery approaches Tates Avenue along the Lisburn Road with an inbound service from Balmoral on 5 June 1948. This was one of 170 trams built by Brush for the system's electrification in 1905. The vast majority survived post-war with a handful surviving into the 1950s. *John Meredith/Online Transport*

For the opening of Belfast's electric tramway, Brush delivered 170 four-wheel open-top cars on Brill 21E trucks in 1905. From 1907, all of the 'Standard Reds', as the type became known, were fitted with open-balcony top covers, but – with the exception of Nos 21/22, 31/35, 78, 123/59/64 that underwent modernisation between 1929 and 1932 – all retained their open vestibules throughout their career. Although a small number had been withdrawn before 1945, the majority of the type survived through to the post-war era, being withdrawn between 1945 and 1951.

21/22, 31/35, 78, 123/59/64/86

In 1929, with the 'Moffett' class having been retrucked, fifty Brush-built Brill 21E 7ft 6in wheelbase trucks were released. The decision was made to utilise these under fifty of the existing 'Standard Reds'; the first to be so treated was No 164 in February 1929. Although forty-one of the trucks were used on Nos 241-91, a further eight older cars – Nos 21/22, 31/35, 78, 123/59/86 – were so treated in a programme that stretched between 1929 and 1932. At the same time, the cars were also rebuilt as fully enclosed by either Sandy Row or by Service Motor Works. The nine rebuilt cars were all withdrawn between 1948 and 1951.

172-74/76-80/82/85/87-89/91/92

Although the original 'Standard Reds' had been built by Brush, the corporation's workshops at Sandy Row built two batches – Nos 171-92 between 1908 and 1910 and Nos 251-91 between 1913 and 1919 – that were fitted with top covers from new. The earlier batch was fitted with Brush-built Brill 21E trucks. One of the type – No 186 – was amongst those cars rebuilt as fully enclosed between 1929 and 1932 but the remainder of the type remained with open vestibules throughout their lives. No 175/81/83/84/90 were withdrawn before 1945 whilst the remaining cars were all taken out of service between 1948 and 1951.

194-200

When, in 1911, the corporation acquired the Cavehill & Whitewell system, it also acquired eight of that operation's ten trams (the remaining two had been sold in 1909 to Mansfield). The ten had originally been built by Brush and were new in 1906. Of the eight, five were short cars originally numbered 1 to 5 and were fitted with Brill trucks; the remaining three were longer cars from the batch numbered 6 to 10. These had been originally fitted with Lycett & Conaty radial trucks. The wheelbase of the longer cars rendered them unsuitable for the corporation routes; as a result, two were rebuilt as standard 28ft cars on Brush Brill-type trucks with third being scrapped. The five smaller cars were also rebuilt as standard cars. Of the six that survived into the post-war era, all were withdrawn for scrap between 1948 and 1951.

Pictured outside Ardoyne depot, No 35 was one of nine of the 'Standard Reds' rebuilt between 1929 and 1932. This was one of the trams rebuilt by the corporation; others were handled by Service Motor Works. *R.W.A. Jones/Online Transport Archive*

Built by the corporation itself on a Brill 21E truck, No 173 was one of 21 'Standard Reds' delivered between 1908 and 1910. A total of 14 survived into 1945 with the last being withdrawn in 1951. *F.N.T. Lloyd-Jones/Online Transport Archive*

Belfast No 197 was one of six cars inherited from the Cavehill & Whitewell system that, having been rebuilt to a style similar to a 'Standard Red', was to see service during the post-war years. *F.N.T. Lloyd-Jones/ Online Transport Archive*

With electrification, the decision was taken eventually to convert fifty horse trams to electric traction. No 247 was one of seven, Nos 244-50, never to receive a balcony top cover, operating as open-top until withdrawal. *F.N.T. Lloyd-Jones/Online Transport Archive*

207/08/12/13/18/20-23/27/32/37/38/44-50
When the Belfast system was electrified, the decision was made that five of the surviving horse trams should be converted for use as electric cars. However, this was eventually extended to include no fewer than fifty of the horse trams, which became Nos 201-50. All received Brush Brill-type four-wheel trucks and their bodies, which had originally been built by the Belfast Street Tramways at Sandy Row, modified. Shorter than the standard cars, the modified trams were to enter service as open-top with open lower-deck vestibules. Most of the trams were eventually to be fitted with lower-deck windscreens and all, apart from Nos 244-50, were to receive open balcony top covers. Nos 247-50 were noticeably different to the other forty-six and may have had a great proportion of new content when built. Of the fifty converted horse cars, thirty – No 201-6/9-11/14-17/19/24-26/28-31/33-36/39-44 – were all withdrawn for scrap between 1931 and 1935 following the introduction of the 'Chamberlain' and McCreary' cars. In later years Nos 213, 244, 249 and 250 were to act as snowploughs, based at Knock, Ardoyne, Sandy Row and Mountpottinger depots respectively. No 243 was used as a railgrinder from 1943. All of the surviving ex-horse trams in passenger service were withdrawn between 1946 and 1951. On closure, No 249 was preserved and is now on display at the Ulster Folk & Transport Museum.

251-91

These forty-one cars were a further batch of corporation-built trams that followed on from Nos 171-92. They were delivered between 1913 and 1919 and were originally fitted with Brush-built Brill 21E four-wheel trucks with a 6ft 6in wheelbase. Following the decision to retruck the 'Moffett' class, fifty Brush-Built Brill 21E 7ft 6in wheelbase trucks were released, of which forty-one were used to retruck this batch of cars between 1929 and 1932. The trams, which had been delivered with top covers but open vestibules, were converted to fully enclosed at the same time, with the work being undertaken either at Sandy Row or at Service Motor Works in Belfast. All of the type were to survive until withdrawals began in

1951; the last were taken out of service in 1954.

292-341

After the First World War there was a need for additional trams and so an order was placed in 1919 for fifty trams from Brush. The first two of these were delivered in December 1920 and all were in service by the middle of the following year. Named the 'Moffett' class after the then general manager, all were fully enclosed from new and supplied with Brush Brill-type 7ft 6in four-wheel trucks. All were subsequently retrucked using Maley & Taunton 8ft 0in swing link trucks; the 7ft 6in trucks thus released were used in the rebuilding of a number of the older trams. All of the class were withdrawn from service between 1951 and 1953 for scrap.

The final 'Standard Reds' were a batch of forty-one delivered between 1913 and 1919, Nos 251-91. These were again rebuilt by either the corporation or by Service Motor Works. No 254, one of those rebuilt by the latter, is seen in the dark blue and cream livery at Bridge End Post Office on the Queens Island route. *R.W.A. Jones/Online Transport Archive*

342-91

Delivered in 1930, the fifty cars of
the 'Chamberlain' class were built by
Brush – Nos 342-81 – and the Belfast-
based Service Motor Works – Nos 382-91;
it is probable that the Belfast-built cars
incorporated parts supplied by Brush. All
were fitted with M&T 8ft 0in swing link
trucks. Withdrawal took place between
1951 and 1954; all were scrapped with
the exception of No 357, which is now
on display at the Ulster Folk & Transport
Museum at Cultra.

392-441

The last new trams acquired by Belfast
Corporation were the fifty 'McCreary'
cars delivered in 1935-36, having been
authorised in late 1934. Built by English
Electric – Nos 392, 423-41 – or Service
Motor Works – Nos 393-422; the latter were
built on underframes supplied by Hurst

Nelson. The fifty cars were all fitted with
M&T 8ft 0in swing link trucks. Initially the
first five cars had problems with dropped
platforms and the later deliveries were
modified to reduce this. The problem was
not, however, wholly resolved and the
structural weakness was one reason why
only ten of the batch survived through
to final closure. All were withdrawn
between 1950 and 1954; none survived into
preservation.

WORKS CARS

The fleet was supplied with two works
cars – Nos A and B – in 1905; these
survived in service until 1930 although
one was not finally scrapped until 1941.
In 1931, a new store car – No 8 – was
constructed by H.M.S. Catherwood, a
local bus operator of Donegall Road,
using the 5ft 6in truck recovered from
withdrawn 'Standard' No 8. No 248 was

The first of the Service Motor Works-built 'Chamberlain' cars, No 382, crosses the complex but partly disused junction at Mountpottinger heading into Mountpottinger Road from Castlereagh Street. At this point, the trams used the trolleybus overhead. *R.W.A. Jones/Online Transport Archive*

One of the fifty 'McCreary' cars, English Electric-built No 426, is seen at the Balmoral terminus of the cross-city route to Ligoniel. Note that the car displays the post-1951 route number (57). *R.W.A. Jones/Online Transport Archive*

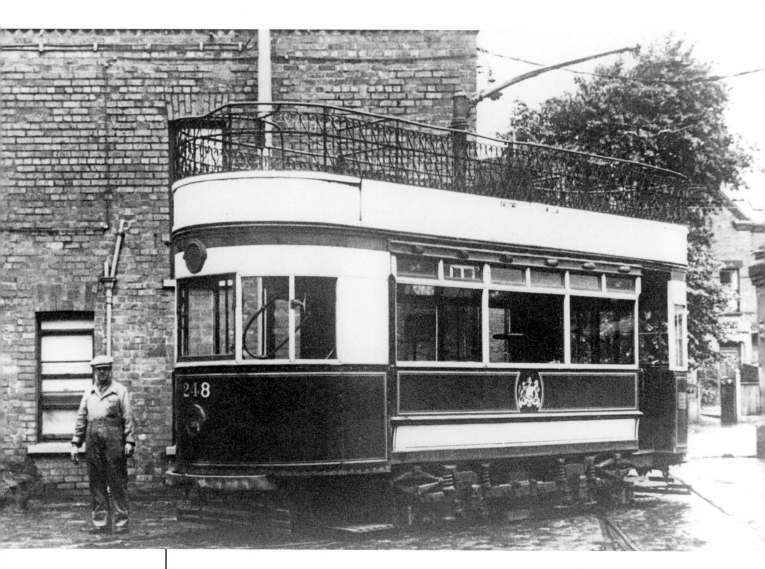

No 248 is recorded after its conversion to a railgrainder; as part of the conversion, one of the staircases was removed. *Barry Cross Collection/Online Transport Archive*

converted into a railgrinder during the war and was fitted with vestibule ends for the purpose, although losing one staircase. It was withdrawn in January 1954. A number of ex-horse cars were employed as snowploughs; each depot had one, the last four being Nos 213 (Knock), 244 (Ardoyne), 249 (Sandy Row) and 250 (Mountpottinger).

A number of other passenger cars, such as Nos 188 (a stores car until withdrawn in 1951 having run with boarded-up windows since wartime damage a decade earlier) and 281/88 (used as breakdown cars from Mountpottinger and Sandy Row), also served as works cars once withdrawn from passenger service.

BESSBROOK & NEWRY

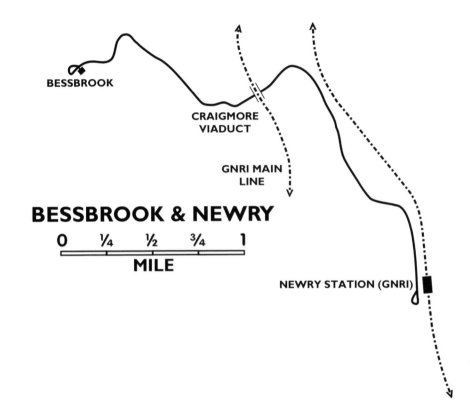

BESSBROOK

CRAIGMORE
VIADUCT

GNRI MAIN
LINE

BESSBROOK & NEWRY

0 ¼ ½ ¾ 1

MILE

NEWRY STATION (GNRI)

Bessbrook & Newry
No 1 pictured with
an enclosed wagon
and trailer No 6;
the latter was built
locally about 1923
and used as the
Richardson family's
private saloon. *Barry
Cross Collection/
Online Transport
Archive*

Bessbrook & Newry No 4 heads away from Bessbrook. Although the line was predominantly third rail, overhead was used when the line crossed public highways. *D.W.K. Jones/NTM*

By the end of the Second World War, the Bessbrook & Newry Tramway was in a relatively parlous condition; as elsewhere, the lack of maintenance was a problem but much more serious for the finances of the line was the competition for the passenger traffic from the frequent bus service operated by the Northern Ireland Road Transport Board.

On 5 October 1947, the tramway issued a new timetable; this was destined to be the last issued and showed only eight workings per day. Three months later – on 10 January 1948 – the last tram operated without due ceremony; the fact that the service was ending was, however, noted, as a local journalist was one of a handful of passengers – the others being a man, woman and child – that travelled on the final departure from

Edward Street. One of the passengers commented: 'I could cry this night. I am on this last run, and I well mind being on the first. I was a wee girl sitting on my father's knee.'

Following the end of services, representatives from the Giant's Causeway inspected the stock with a view to supplementing their own equipment but decided against purchase. One car, No 2, was however secured, acquired by the Manchester-based Mather & Platt, where it was initially refurbished for use as a cricket hut. Fully restored, it is now on display at Cultra.

DEPOT

The Bessbrook & Newry was served by a single depot, located at Bessbrook and opened with the line in 1885 and closed on 10 January 1948. At the time of writing, the building is still extant, one of the few physical remains of this pioneering electric line other than some sections of the trackbed.

CLOSURES
10 January 1948   Bessbrook to Newry

FLEET
All of the tramway's passenger cars operational in 1945 were to survive through to the line's final closure in January 1948. One of the motor cars was initially preserved and, subsequently, a trailer car has been secured and is currently undergoing restoration.

1/4
In 1920, Hurst Nelson supplied two single-deck trams that were both fitted with maximum traction bogies. It is believed that No 4 incorporated parts from the original No 1 of 1885, which was withdrawn contemporaneously with the delivery of the two new trams. No 1 could accommodate forty passengers whilst No 4, which also included a luggage compartment, could only accommodate

thirty-two. The original No 1 had been built by the Ashbury Carriage Co of Manchester and provided accommodation for twenty-four second-class and ten first-class passengers.

2
In 1928, the Bessbrook & Newry acquired two single-deck trailers from the closed Dublin & Lucan. No 24 was to become Bessbrook & Newry No 7, having been regauged from 3ft 6in to 3ft 0in and could accommodate twenty-six passengers. In 1942, the body of No 7 was placed on the underframes of the original No 2 and extended to form a new No 2, on maximum traction bogies. Following the line's closure, No 2 was acquired by the Manchester company of Mather & Platt for display at its works; following the establishment of a transport museum in Belfast in 1955, it returned to Northern Ireland. It is now displayed at Cultra. The original No 2 had also been built by the Ashbury Carriage Co but was shorter than No 1 and accommodated only second-class passengers

Bessbrook & Newry
No 4 was one of two single-deck trams supplied by Hurst Nelson in 1920. It is pictured in front of the line's depot at Bessbrook. *Barry Cross Collection/ Online Transport Archive*

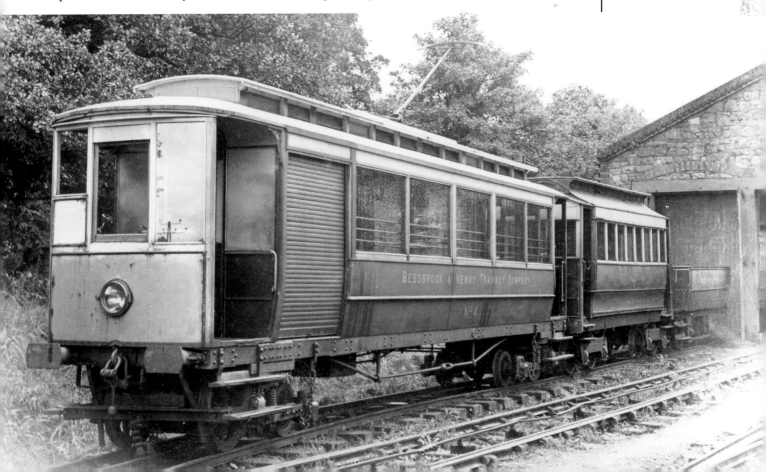

Bessbrook & Newry
No 2 represented a combination of the body of one of the ex-Dublin & Lucan trailers with the underframes from the original No 2. The 'new' tram entered service in 1942. *F.N.T. Lloyd-Jones/Online Transport Archive*

3
This was an unpowered trailer car that was supplied by Starbuck for the line's opening in 1885. It provided seating accommodation for forty-four passengers

4
This was Hurst Nelson-built car that dated originally to 1920. When new it was fitted with the bogies salvaged from the original No 1, but these were replaced in 1927.

5
This single-deck bogie trailer car was originally Dublin & Lucan No 27 and dated to when its original owner was a 3ft 0in gauge steam operated line. Converted to 3ft 6in when the Dublin & Lucan was electrified, the trailer was re-converted to 3ft 0in when sold to the Bessbrook & Newry in 1928. Originally numbered 8 by

the Bessbrook & Newry, it was renumbered 5 in 1942. It could accommodate twenty-four passengers. It is believed that, like No 2, it operated in the Dublin & Lucan livery for a brief period on the Bessbrook & Newry.

6
This was a four-wheel trailer car built locally in about 1923. Seating a maximum of twelve passengers, the car was used as the Richardson family's private saloon. After closure, the body of No 6 was acquired by the Convent of Mercy in Bessbrook for use as a summer house. It has been secured for preservation.

7
This was a small open unpowered trailer car that was supplied by Hurst Nelson in 1920. Originally No 5, it was renumbered in 1942.

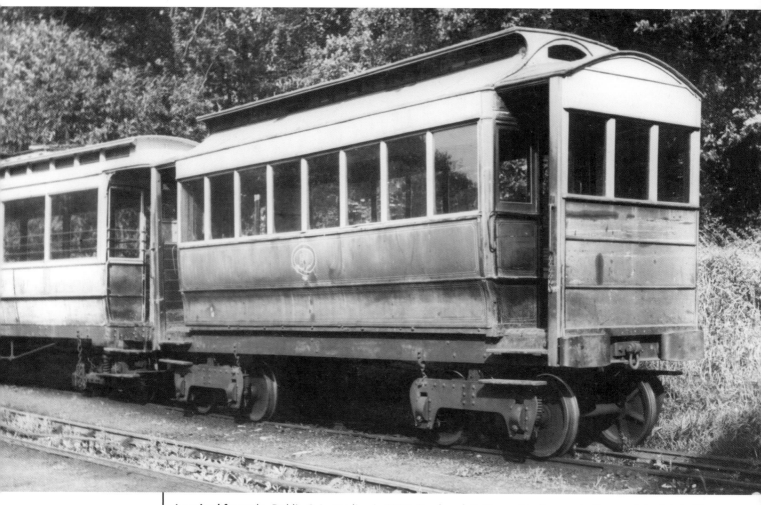

Acquired from the Dublin & Lucan line in 1928, Bessbrook & Newry No 5 was a trailer car. It is pictured here still in its Dublin & Lucan livery of green and cream, in which it operated for a number of years and prior to modification in which alternative windows were blanked out. *W.A. Camwell/NTM*

Bessbrook & Newry trailer car No 6 was constructed locally in the early 1920s and was used as the Richardson family's private saloon. *Barry Cross Collection/ Online Transport Archive*

CARDIFF

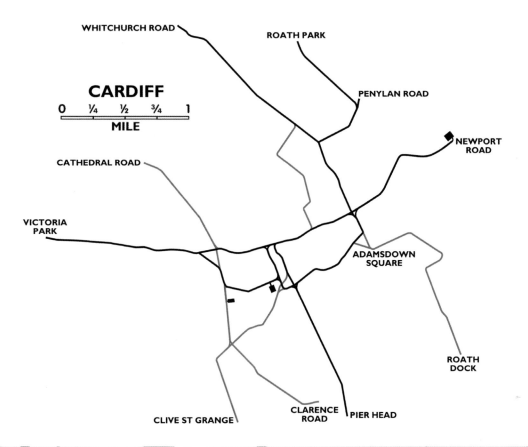

WHITCHURCH ROAD

ROATH PARK

CARDIFF

0   ¼   ½   ¾   1
MILE

PENYLAN ROAD

NEWPORT
ROAD

CATHEDRAL ROAD

VICTORIA
PARK

ADAMSDOWN
SQUARE

ROATH
DOCK

CLIVE ST GRANGE

CLARENCE
ROAD

PIER HEAD

Pictured towards the end of its life, No 84, recorded outside the depot at Roath on 13 August 1946, was one of a handful of open-top trams to survive in Cardiff after the war. Beyond the depot can be seen the corporation power station; this was constructed alongside the depot in order to provide the necessary power for the new electric trams in the early twentieth century. *Ian L. Wright/Online Transport Archive*

On 25 May 1945, Cardiff No 92 stands at the Whitchurch Road terminus; this was destined to be the last tram service operated in Cardiff five years later. Note the PAYE notice and the white-painted wartime bumper. *Ian L. Wright/Online Transport Archive*

The first post-war conversion in Cardiff was on 27 April 1946 when the service from Hayes Bridge to Pier Head. Here No 3 and 105 are seen at the Pier Head terminus on the last day of route 16. *Ian L. Wright/Online Transport Archive*

An impressive line-up of trams, including Nos 11 and 65, stand at the Victoria Park terminus on 25 March 1946. Services were withdrawn from Victoria Park during 1948. *Ian L. Wright/ Online Transport Archive*

The Newport Road route ceased to be operated by trams on 17 October 1948 although the track and overhead remained intact in order to access the depot at Roath. Here No 88, used for an LRTL tour, stands on the depot fan at Roath on 27 March 1949. The terminus of the Newport Road routes was slightly to the west of the dept. Sadly attempts to preserve this tram failed. *Ian L. Wright/ Online Transport Archive*

Cardiff No 56 stands at the terminus of the terminus at Roath Park on 19 February 1945. There was a small turning circle at this terminus and note the tram shelter in the middle distance. This service ceased on 5 December 1949. *Ian L. Wright/Online Transport Archive*

The last Cardiff tram to operate, suitably decorated, was No 11 on 20 February 1950; here the car is pictured on Newport Road in front of Roath depot. *R. W. A. Jones/Online Transport Archive*

This souvenir ticket was issued on the last Electric Tramcar operated in the City of Cardiff.

Good-bye my friends, this is the end ;

I've travelled miles and miles.

And watched your faces through the years,

Show anger, tears and smiles.

Although you've criticised my looks—

and said I was too slow,

I got you there and brought you back,

through rain and sleet and snow.

20th February, 1950.

L T
Last Tram

8309

SOUVENIR TICKET

CARDIFF CORPORATION TRANSPORT DEPARTMENT

3D.

1902
to
1950

JOURNEY NUMBER

1 2 3 4 5 6 7 8 9 10 11 12 13 14

ISSUED SUBJECT TO THE BYE-LAWS AND REGULATIONS

NOT TRANSFERABLE

THIS TICKET MUST BE SHOWN ON DEMAND

Service No. 1 – St. Mary St. & Whitchurch Rd.

OUTWARD
INWARD

Bell Punch Company, Limited, London.

CARDIFF TRANSPORT

CORPORATION DEPARTMENT

The Chairman of the Transport Committee (Councillor J. P. Collins) invites you to accompany him on the Last Journey to be operated by an Electric Tramcar in the City of Cardiff on

MONDAY, 20TH FEBRUARY, 1950

ASSEMBLE 7.0 P.M.
WHITCHURCH ROAD TRAM TERMINUS

LIGHT REFRESHMENTS
R.S.V.P.

Following the introduction of trolleybuses in 1942, Cardiff's tram network in 1945 covered Victoria Park to the west, Whitchurch Road and Roath Park to the north, Newport Road to the east and Pier Head to the south. The network was operated by a fleet of almost ninety trams, the majority of which were fully-enclosed four-wheel lowbridge cars built in the early 1920s. During the war, the tramway suffered some damage and a number of trams were repainted in a grey livery.

One unusual aspect of the Cardiff system was the use of PAYE equipment, using patented coinboxes. The system had been designed by the chief engineer, William J. Evans, with the assistance of East Lancashire Coachbuilders. The system was first used with the new trolleybuses on 1 March 1942. In order to use PAYE equipment on the trams, the routes were reorganised from 3 May 1942 so that all now terminated in the centre. From this date, the tram routes were numbered as follows: 1A/1B – Whitchurch Road; 2A/2B – Newport Road; 4A/4B – Roath Park; 5A – St Mary Street to Victoria Park; 8 – Windsor Place to Victoria Park; and, 16 – The Hayes to Pier Head. PAYE equipment was introduced to all tram routes between March 1943 and August the same year. The use of PAYE equipment was highlighted by a board in the windscreens of the trams.

In 1946, John W. Dunning became general manager; prior to that date he had been traffic manager and, since the death of the previous general manager (William Forbes in 1940), he and Evans had jointly run the operation. The policy of the corporation was to convert the remaining trams to trolleybus operation. The first route under consideration was that to Pier Head, where the condition of the track was giving concern. The corporation was faced by the need either to relay the track or replace the trams; although an order for single-deck trolleybuses was placed, such were the post-war constraints for vehicle delivery that it was considered unlikely that these would be delivered

until 1948/49. As a result, it was decided to convert the Pier Head route to bus, with the last trams operating on 27 April 1946. Second-hand single-deck trolleybuses acquired from Pontypridd permitted conversion of the route to trolleybus on 17 August 1947. Also in 1946, the track in Clare Street, Lower Cathedral Road and Neville Street was closed; Clare Road depot, with the track along Wood Street, was to close to trams on 25 August 1946.

As the post-war vehicle problems diminished so it became possible to continue the process of trolleybus conversion. The next route to be converted was that to Victoria Park. Trams were replaced on this corridor in two phases; on 5 June 1948 trams ceased to operate the Windsor Place to Victoria Park service (route 8) and on 5 June 1948 they were withdrawn from route 5A (Victoria Park to St Mary Street). Trolleybuses took over operation of the route on 4 July 1948.

Although, since the closure of Clare Road depot, all trams were housed at Roath depot at the end of the Newport Road route, the next routes to be converted were the 2A and 2B; these were replaced by bus on 16 October 1948 with trolleybuses taking over two years later. The corporation hoped that the final conversion would take place during the summer of 1949; however, two factors prevented this happening. Firstly, the ongoing delays in the delivery of new trolleybuses meant that there were not enough replacement vehicles and, secondly, the need to lower the roadway under the railway bridges at Queen Street to create a headroom of 16ft 6in for the new trolleybuses.

Work on the latter commenced on 12 July 1949; it was decided not to retain the tram track under the bridges but to divert the remaining routes – Whitchurch Road and Roath Park – via the track in Moira Terrace, Adam Street and Bute Terrace that had been retained as a diversionary route following the conversion of the Roath Dock route before the war. This use of this track – which was in good condition – resulted in the closure of much of the existing city centre track (Queen Street, Duke Street, High Street and The Hayes plus much of St Mary Street). The work on lowering the roadway was completed on 27 October 1949.

With work completed, the corporation moved swiftly to eliminate its final trams, of which only twenty-nine remained in service. On 3 December 1949, trams operated the Roath Park service for the last time; the last car on the route was No 107, which departed from Roath Park at 11.10pm. The final route – Whitchurch Road – operated for the last time on Sunday 19 February 1950, with No 112, suitably inscribed, as the last service car at 10.45pm. On Monday 20 February, No 11, decorated for the occasion, made farewell trips along the route with No 112 providing additional capacity; No 11 then made its final run, with civic party on board, that evening.

Of the Cardiff fleet, no passenger car was preserved but works car No 131 was secured; it is now part of the NTM collection at Crich.

DEPOTS
Two depots survived the Second World War to serve Cardiff's tramcar fleet. The smaller of the two was Clare Road, which opened originally in 1902 and in 1942 was partially converted to accommodate trolleybuses. Trams ceased to use the depot from 25 August 1946. The main depot and workshops were located at Roath adjacent to the corporation's power station. This opened on 18 September 1902 and was to survive until the final closure of the system on 19 February 1950. There were also three depots – Severn Road (closed 17 October 1902), Harbour Road (10 February 1903) and Lucas Street (17 October 1902) – that closed as the horse trams were withdrawn and one – Wood Street – that was converted from a horse to electric depot, which closed just before the start of the Second World War.

CLOSURES

27 April 1946	16 – Hayes Bridge to Pier Head
24 January 1948	8 – Windsor Place to Victoria Park
5 June 1948	5A – Victoria Park to St Mary Street
16 October 1948	2A/2B – St Mary Street to Newport Road
5 December 1949	4A/4B – Roath Street to St Mary Street
19 February 1950	1A/1B – Whitchurch Road to St Mary Street

1-4, 7-9, 11/14/16-21/25-28, 31/33/35-40, 55-60/62-71/73-75/77/79-83/85-89, 91-98, 100-14
One of the problems with the Cardiff system was the number of low railway bridges; this precluded the operation of conventional enclosed double-deck trams. However, Brush had patented a fully-enclosed lowbridge double-deck tram, using a conventional Peckham P22 four-wheel truck but with smaller diameter wheels, and in November 1922 the then general manager, R.L. Horsfield, was authorised to purchase one. No 101 was completed in March 1923 and suitably impressed the Tramways Committee with the result that a further eighty of the type were ordered in three batches. The first nine cars were delivered in December 1923 and all were in service by October 1925. Of the Brush-built cars, all were to survive the war with the exception of No 78, which was dismantled for spares in 1940. Five more were broken up in early 1947 following accident damage; these were Nos 7, 21, 62, 89 and 98. The remainder were withdrawn as the system contracted and scrapped. None was to survive into preservation.

22/23/29, 30/32/34, 84, 90
For the introduction of electric tramcar services in Cardiff, ERTCW supplied a number of trams – bogie and four-wheel, double- and single-deck. No 21-40 and 75-94 were open-top and uncanopied double-deck cars fitted with Brill

The majority of the Cardiff fleet post-war were fully-enclosed double-deckers such as No 1 seen here on Adam Street approaching one of the numerous low railway bridges that had such an impact on tramcar development in the city. This section, retained for emergency use in 1936, was to see increased use following the diversion of routes 1 and 4 on 11 July 1949. *R.W.A. Jones/ Online Transport Archive*

22E maximum traction bogies. Of these, Nos 22-24/29, 30/32/34, 76, 84 and 90 were rebuilt with canopies and enclosed lower-deck platforms in 1921 (No 24) and 1922 (remainder). The unrebuilt cars were largely withdrawn as the new Brush built were delivered between 1923 and 1925. Two of the rebuilt cars – Nos 24 and 76 – did not survive to 1945 but the remaining open-top cars survived into 1946 in use on peak-hour services between Victoria Park and Newport Road; the last were withdrawn during 1946 and scrapped.

Apart from the fully-enclosed cars, eight open-top cars, including No 84 seen on Newport Road on 13 August 1946, were retained. These were all withdrawn during 1946. *Ian L. Wright/Online Transport Archive*

Works car No 131 dated originally to 1902. Preserved following withdrawal, it is seen here at the Talygarn Street crossover on Sunday morning whilst undertaking railgrinding duties on 31 March 1946. *Ian L. Wright/Online Transport Archive*

131

Constructed by ERTCW on a Brill 21E four-wheel truck, No 131 was built as a water car cum sweeper in 1902. Unnumbered between 1902 and 1905 and again from 1926 to 1949, the car was to survive until final closure in 1950. Preserved on withdrawal, No 131 is now fully restored as part of the National Tramway Museum Collection at Crich.

DOUGLAS

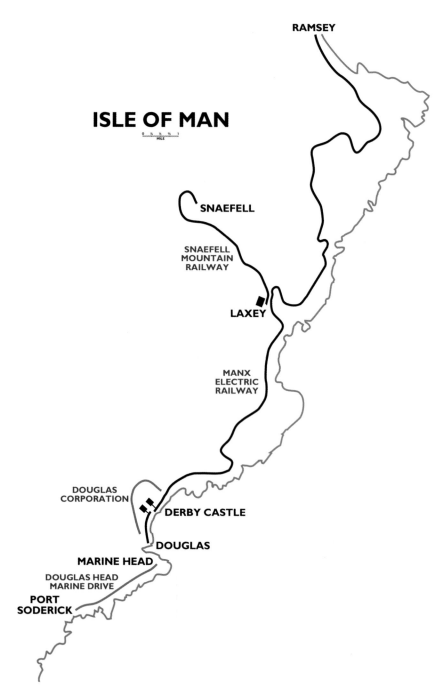

ISLE OF MAN

RAMSEY

SNAEFELL

SNAEFELL
MOUNTAIN
RAILWAY

LAXEY

MANX
ELECTRIC
RAILWAY

DOUGLAS
CORPORATION

DERBY CASTLE

DOUGLAS

MARINE HEAD

DOUGLAS HEAD
MARINE DRIVE

PORT
SODERICK

S ince 1927, the Douglas horse tramway operated during the summer months only and so services had ceased for the year on 30 September 1939; it was to be almost seven years before they resumed. The first trams to operate post-war took to the streets on 22 May 1946. The fleet comprised more than forty single and double-deck trams with forty-two replacement horses acquired from Ireland. This was in contrast to the 135 horses owned by the corporation in 1935.

The future of the tramways was in some doubt, however, and pressure for abandonment developed as financial pressures increased as a result of declining usage. Although a motion calling for conversion was defeated by twenty-one votes to one in November 1947, savings were to be made. In 1948 and 1949 all the remaining double-deck trams, with the exception of No 14, were withdrawn; this was followed in 1952 by the withdrawal of six single-deck trams – Nos 9, 19, 20 and 23-25 with No 30 following in 1954 – and the transfer of No 14 to the Museum of British Transport at Clapham in 1955.

Following its reintroduction and as a result of the savings in maintenance, the number of horses and the reduction in the operational fleet, the horse tramway remained generally profitable, reaching a maximum profit of £6,377 in 1955. The corporation-owned buses were less successful and the profits from the trams were used to subsidise the buses. However, this could not continue as the tramway profits declined to £1,794 in 1959 and to a loss the following year. The deteriorating financial position – despite fare increases which could only be sanctioned by the Manx parliament

On 21 September 1974 Nos 45 and 46 pass on the Promenade; of the two, only No 45 remains with the operator and No 46 was preserved in England until 2001. *Barry Cross Collection/ Online Transport Archive*

In May 1953 one of the three trams supplied by Milnes Voss between 19019 and 1911 is pictured at the southern terminus of the line; No 47 was to be withdrawn in 1978 and is now based at the museum at Jurby. *Jim Jarvis/Online Transport Archive*

On 16 September 2000, Douglas No 40 stands on the traverser outside the historic Strathallan Crescent depot. Home of the fleet since 1896, the depot is now under threat as plans are afoot for its replacement. No 40 was one of the horse trams sold in August 2016 as part of a fleet reduction programme. *Author*

following a statute of 1895 – again led to pressure for the tramway's abandonment but these were rejected.

In 1968, following two decades of purchasing horses from Ireland, the first English-bred horses post-war were acquired; thereafter, for a number of years until the costs made Manx-bred horses the preferred option, new horses were sourced from both Ireland and England on an annual basis.

The following year saw the Duke of Edinburgh take the reins of No 44 during a royal visit to the island. In August 1972, the same tram was used by the Queen when she visited Douglas. Reputedly, this was the first time that the monarch had travelled by tram. The visit in 1972

resulted in an interesting conundrum. It transpired that the corporation's armorial bearings were not officially sanctioned by the College of Arms, nor were they likely to be approved. The corporation thus faced the cost of redesigning and registering a set of new arms. However, to avoid the cost, the corporation simply redesignated the existing bearings as the Corporate Common Seal of the Borough.

The financial position of the operation deteriorated in the early 1970s, with a record loss of £13,170 being recorded in 1974 and the second half of the decade saw the fleet continue to shrink. No 26 was withdrawn in 1974, and Nos 11 and 22 following in 1976 whilst No 47 succumbed two years later. In 1976, the tramway celebrated its centenary, with double-deck car No 14 returning to the island and a celebratory parade being held on 9 August, whilst ownership of the bus fleet was merged with that of the Isle of Man Road Services, leaving the corporation to operate the horse tramway alone. Three further withdrawals occurred in 1980, with the sale of Nos 48-50 to the Manx Electric Railway.

In the spring of 1983, No 1 was transferred briefly to England for use by Sealink for promotional purposes; it was to return to Douglas on 12 March 1983. The same year saw Nos 11 and 47 transferred to the museum at Ramsey and No 10 withdrawn. The tramway's losses continued to mount, reaching £18,000 in 1974 despite carrying 500,000 passengers. One success was the use of No 14 for private charter work; as a result, it was decided in 1985 to restore No 18 to its original double-deck condition. The work was completed in 1989. The fleet was further reduced by the withdrawal in 1987 of Nos 31 and 46 and in 1991 by the withdrawal of No 41. For a brief period, No 46 was transferred after withdrawal to a children's playground but was subsequently rescued and transferred for preservation in England on 21 March 1988.

During 1993, the tramway's manager, Wilson Gibb, retired; he was not directly replaced with control of the route being shared between the station superintendent and stable foreman. Although 1993 was designated the Isle of Man 'Year of the Railways', in order to encourage additional traffic, the horse tramway's turnover was £190,000 resulting in a loss of £108,000 for the year. This again resulted in discussions about the line's future. The following year saw a change to the tickets, with the legend 'Douglas Borough Council Tramway' replacing the familiar 'Douglas Corporation Tramway'.

Over recent years, the future of the tramway has been uncertain. Partly this is due to a desire to rebuild the Promenade and transfer the trams from their existing location to run alongside the road and partly due to deteriorating finances. In 2015, the tramway lost £263,000 with the result that Douglas Corporation announced that services would not resume for the 2016 season and that the fleet would be dispersed to museums. This led to an outcry and Tynwald established a committee to see what, if any, future there was.

This led to the operation of the line being taken over by the Isle of Man Heritage Railways, a division of the Manx Department of Infrastructure, and services operated again during the 2016 and 2017 seasons. However, the fleet has been significantly reduced, with six trams – Nos 28, 33, 34, 37, 39 and 40 – being sold at auction on 27 August 2016, leaving serving services to be operated by thirteen trams – Nos 1, 12, 18, 21, 27, 29, 32, 36, 38 and 42-45. Whether it was the perceived threat to the line or not, but the 2016 season saw an almost fifty per cent increase in passengers using the line as the tramway celebrated its 140th anniversary – something that few expected to see following the line's abrupt closure at the end of 2015.

On 17 January 2017, Tynwald voted to retain the full length of the horse tramway although some of the route, between Derby Castle and Broadway, was to be singled. There had been earlier proposals, only narrowly rejected, that would have seen the line curtailed with the loss of the section from Villa Marina to Sea Terminal.

DEPOTS

The home for the Douglas horse tram fleet since 1896 has been the depot at Strathallan Crescent, at the northern end of the line. The horse tramway had been extended to this point in late 1890. Prior to its demolition in 1990, the erstwhile cable tram depot at York Road, in Douglas had been used for the storage of withdrawn horse trams prior to their disposal. The depot was also used for the repair of the horse trams — moved there by low-loader — until the 1980s. Prior to the opening of Strathallan Crescent, the tram fleet had been accommodated in Douglas town centre at a depot built at Burnt Hill Mill. Towards the end of 2016 it was announced that a new temporary facility was to be built, subject to planning consent (which was given in early 2017), on the site of Summerland to replace the existing depot, which was deemed beyond economic repair, and the stables at Summer Hill.

FLEET
Cars marked * are still in service or in store with the operator at the time of writing.

1*
The second Douglas tram to carry to number 1 was built by Milnes-Voss in 1913 and replaced a double-deck tram that has been withdrawn in 1900. The enclosed saloon, which seats thirty, remains in service.

2, 3, 5, 6, 8
The Starbuck Car & Wagon Co Ltd manufactured seven open-top double-deck trams for Douglas in 1876 (Nos 1-3) and 1884 (Nos 5-8) in 1884. Two of the cars were withdrawn relatively early: No 1 in 1900 and No 7 in 1924. The remaining five were withdrawn for scrap in 1948 (Nos 2, 3 and 5) and 1949 (Nos 6 and 8).

4
In 1882 the original three Starbuck-built cars were supplemented by a single open-top double-deck car built by the Metropolitan Carriage & Wagon Co Ltd. This car was scrapped in 1949.

9-11
In 1886 three open toast-racks were supplied; although these had been ordered from Starbuck, the trio may actually have been built by G.F. Milnes & Co following the demise of the Starbuck company. Of these, No 9 was scrapped in 1952, No 10 in 1983 and No 11 was preserved following withdrawal in 1976.

Douglas No 1, built by Milnes in 1913, stands outside the depot at Strathallan Crescent. *F. K. Farrell/ Online Transport Archive*

One of the few double-deck trams to survive post-war in Douglas, No 2 was scrapped in 1948. *Martin Jenkins Collection/Online Transport Archive*

No 9, seen here derelict at Summer Hill depot on 13 August 1947, was one of three open toast-racks built in 1886; it was eventually scrapped in 1952. *John Meredith/Online Transport Archive)*

12*

Supplied by the Starbuck Car & Wagon Co of Birkenhead, No 12 was new in 1888. This toastrack car is now the oldest surviving operational tram in the fleet.

14/15/18*

In 1887, six double-deck cars were acquired from the South Shields Tramways Co; these had originally been built by the Metropolitan Railway Carriage & Wagon Co of Birmingham in 1883 with the exception of No 18, which was built by the Falcon Engine & Car Works Co of Loughborough. Numbered 13-18 on the Isle of Man, No 13 was renumbered 14 when the original No 14 was scrapped in 1908. Nos 16 and 17 were scrapped in 1915 and 1917. On withdrawal in 1949 the new No 14 was preserved and was displayed in England as part of the BTC collection from 1955 before returning to the Isle of Man in 1976. It has been displayed at the Manx Museum in Douglas since 1990. No 15 was also withdrawn in 1949 but scrapped. No 18 was converted to single-deck in 1904 but was restored to original double-deck condition in 1989. It is the only extant double-deck horse tram in the fleet.

19, 20

These two cars were both supplied as open toast-rack cars by G.F. Milnes & Co in 1886. They were both withdrawn for scrap in 1952.

21*/22

In 1890 G.F. Milnes & Co supplied two open toast-rack trams. In 1908, No 22 was converted into a sunshade or umbrella car, in which guise it was to operate until withdrawal in 1976. Thereafter it was used for a period as a mobile shop at Strathallan Crescent until it was transferred to the museum at Jurby.

Douglas No 18 was one of six double-deck cars acquired from South Shields in 1886. This was converted to single-deck in 1904 – the only one of the sextet so treated – but was to be restored to original condition in 1989. *F.K. Farrell/Online Transport Archive*

23
This open toastrack car was delivered by G.F. Milnes & Co in 1891; fitted with a retractable canvas roof in 1908 and a fixed roof during the 1920s (as a further umbrella or sunshade car), the car was to survive through until being withdrawn for scrap in 1952.

24-26
Three further open toast-rack cars were supplied by G.F. Milnes & Co in 1892. No 24 ws a third tram to receive a retractable canvas roof in 1908 and a fixed roof during the 1920s. Whilst Nos 24 and 25 were sold for scrap in 1952, No 26 was to soldier on until being withdrawn and scrapped in 1974.

27*/28/29*
Three closed thirty-seat winter saloon cars, Nos 27-29, were supplied by

G.F. Milnes & Co in 1892. All three survived until the summer of 2016 when No 28 was sold at auction on 27 August. Of the six cars sold on this occasion, No 28 raised the most – £2,800 – when sold but, at the time of writing, its final destination is unknown.

30/31
G.F. Milnes & Co supplied a further two open toast-rack cars, Nos 30 and 31, in 1894. These could seat thirty-eight passengers; No 30 was withdrawn and scrapped in 1952 whilst No 31 was to survive until 1987, having been used between 1968 and 1975 as an advertising tram.

32*/33/34/35*/36*/37
In 1896, the fleet was further increased by the acquisition of six further covered toast-racks, Nos 32-37. In 1908 the process

Originally an open toast-rack car, No. 22 was fitted with a retractable canvas cover in 1908 and a fixed roof during the 1920s to become an umbrella or sunshade car. Withdrawn in 1976, it was preserved after a period in use as a mobile shop. *Phil Tatt/Online Transport Archive*

Douglas No 26 was one of a trio supplied in 1892; the last of the three to survive, it was finally scrapped in 1976. *Barry Cross Collection/Online Transport Archive*

In service until sold at auction as part of a fleet reduction exercise in the summer of 2016, No 28 was one of three saloons delivered in 1892. *Phil Tatt/Online Transport Archive*

Pictured at Derby Castle on 13 August 1947, No 30 was one of two toast-rack cars supplied in 1894; it survived until 1954. *John Meredith/Online Transport Archive*

New in 1896, No 34 was one of three of the batch to be sold by the operator following the auction of surplus trams in August 2016. *Phil Tatt/Online Transport Archive*

of fitting bulkheads to the batch was started; it was not completed until 1968 when No 33 was the last to be so treated. All survived with the operator until the decision in the summer of 2016 that the fleet be reduced. Nos 33, 34 and 37 were sold at auction on 27 August 2016; at the time of writing their final destination is unknown

38*/39/40

G.F. Milnes & Co built a further batch of three open toast-rack cars, Nos 38-40, in 1905. These provide seating for forty passengers. Two of the cars, Nos 39 and 40, were also sold at auction on 27 August 2016. No 39 was acquired for preservation on the island by the Manx Electric Railway Society whilst No 40's final destination is unknown at present.

Also a victim of the fleet reduction process in August 2016, No 40 was one of three cars supplied in 1905. *Phil Tatt/ Online Transport Archive*

41/42*

Milnes-Voss supplied two open toast-rack cars in 1905. No 41 was withdrawn in 1988 and scrapped.

43*/44*

In 1907 UEC delivered two covered toast-racks with a seating capacity of 40. No 44 is regarded as the royal tram, having carried members of the royal family on visits to the town.

45*/46/47

Between 1909 and 1911 Milnes Voss & Co Ltd delivered three covered toast-racks to Douglas; these could seat forty-four. No 47 was withdrawn in 1978 and preserved; it is now based at the Jurby museum. No 46 was withdrawn in 1987 and eventually preserved in England; it was based at Birkenhead until scrapped in 2001. No 45 remains in service.

Built in 1905, No 41 is seen at Walpole Avenue on 13 August 1947. The tram was scrapped in 1991.
John Meredith/Online Transport Archive

Pictured at Strathallan Crescent on 8 April 1950, No 43 remains in service at the time of writing. *Tony Wickens/Online Transport Archive*

On 7 June 1965, No 45 passes the Castle Hotel and the now-demolished Palace Theatre. No 45 was one of three trams supplied by Milnes Voss & Co Ltd between 1909 and 1911; it is the only one of the trio still in service. *W.J.Wyse/ LRTA (London Area) Collection/Online Transport Archive*

48-50

In 1935, three convertible saloons were built by the Vulcan Motor & Engineering Co. These seated thirty-eight or forty-four, depending how they were configured. In 1979, the three trams were modified from convertible to all-weather format, to permit a five-minute frequency of service in bad weather. They were, however, not destined to survive much longer. All three were sold for use as shelters by the MER in 1980; however, only No 49 was so used and was rescued for display in Ramsey in 1982. Nos 48 and 50 were scrapped the same year.

Douglas No 50 was one of three trams supplied in 1935 – the last new trams acquired by the operator. It was one of three sold to the MER in 1980 and subsequently scrapped. *John Meredith/ Online Transport Archive*

DUBLIN

On 25 September 1948 No 296 stands at Dalkey with a route 8 service heading back towards the city centre. This was one of twenty 'Luxury' – as they were known by enthusiasts but not officially – bogie trams built between 1931 and 1936; all bar one were to survive through until the system's final closure. *Ian L. Wright/ Online Transport Archive*

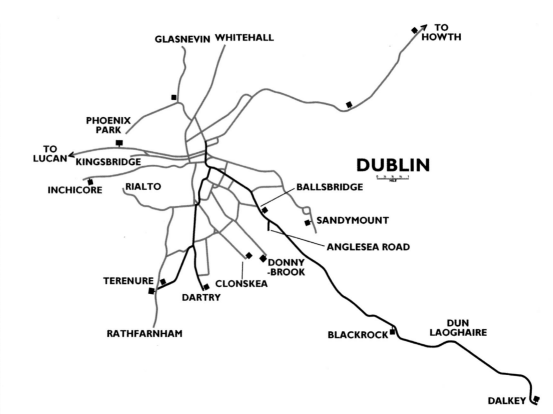

Nelson Pillar in central Dublin was the focal point of the DUT network and here Nos 178 on route 15, 9 on route 14, and 93 and 282 on route 8 await their next duties. *F. N. T. Lloyd-Jones/ Online Transport Archive*

'Luxury Car' No 205 stands at the terminus of route 14 at Dartry. Note, in the foreground, the crude work undertaken to the road following the removal of the track that once served the depot on the left. *F.N.T. Lloyd-Jones/Online Transport Archive*

Amongst the last new Dublin trams constructed in 1936 was 'Luxury' No 102; the car is pictured here in bound on a route 15 service from Terenure. This route was converted to bus operation on 31 October 1948. *F.N.T. Lloyd-Jones/ Online Transport Archive*

As late as 1937, the tramway system in Dublin was substantially intact and a significant number of new trams had been constructed over the previous decade. There had been some minor abandonments but there was no overall plan for conversion although the portion of route 21 from College Green to Westland Row had been withdrawn on 17 February 1937.

This was, however, to change following a board meeting on 1 March 1938 at which the directors decided on a policy of tramway abandonment in favour of the diesel bus. The first closure, from Sandymount Green to Sandymount Tower (route 3) on 7 February 1938, had already taken place. The 1905 extension to Rialto from Dolphin's Barn followed on 28 February 1938; albeit announced initially as a temporary suspension as a result of public works; services were never resumed.

The first conversions in accordance with the new policy occurred on 16 April 1938 with routes 23 (Parkgate Street to Ballybough) and 24 (Parkgate Street to O'Connell Bridge) operating for the last time. The final conversion of 1938 took place on 1 June, with buses taking over operation of route 30 (Nelson Pillar to Dollymount).

New Year's Day 1939 saw the next conversion with the demise of route 12 (Nelson Pillar to Palmerston Park). This was followed on 5 March by the elimination of the 19/20 (Dolphin's Barn to Glasnevin) and on 1 May by the routes 16/17 (Rathfarnham to Whitehall and Terenure to Whitehall respectively) along with the northern section of route 11 (to Whitehall) and route 1 (Nelson Pillar to Ringsend) although the latter did not involve any track abandonment. The southern section of route 11 (Clonksea) was converted on 2 July 1939. The outbreak

One of the 'Luxury' bogie cars, No 300, heads inbound over one of the sections of interlaced track on Lower George Street, Dun Laoghaire, with a route 7 service on 25 September 1948. *Ian L. Wright/Online Transport Archive*

of war in September 1939 caused a number of tramways in the UK to defer closure plans; this was not, however, the position in Dublin where DUT decided to maintain its policy despite the potential threat caused by reliance upon imported fuel.

The next casualty was route 21 (College Green to Inchicore) which was last operated by trams on 4 February 1940. This was followed on 26 March 1940 by the service 2 (Nelson Pillar to Sandymount Green). This was followed on 13 April by routes 25 and 26 (O'Connell Bridge to Lucan and Chapelizod respectively) and on 2 June by routes 9 and 10 (Donnybrook to Phoenix Park); the remainder of route 9 (to Phoenix Park via Dawson Street) was converted on 6 June. The last conversion of 1940 occurred on 1 December with the demise of route 18 (Kenilworth Square to Lansdowne Road).

Following agreement with the Clontarf & Hill of Howth company, for whom DUT operated the service through to Howth, the 31 (Nelson Pillar to Howth) was converted on 31 March 1941. Reflecting the company's change of emphasis, it was officially renamed Dublin United Transport in the same month. The closure process had reduced the once significant system to five services but these would survive until towards the end of the decade.

As the war progressed so the problems with maintaining the country's infrastructure increased. This was compounded by a severe drought which caused a massive reduction in electricity; at the time, most of Ireland's electricity was generated via the hydroelectric scheme on the River Shannon at Ardnacrusha. The drought reduced the waterflow and thus the amount of power generated; from 1 April 1944 tram services in Dublin ceased after 9.30pm each evening and subsequently were withdrawn completely. This led to rumours that the trams had operated for the final time; however, these proved to be false and the trams were restored to service on 22 October 1944. The bus substitution involved the hire of vehicles from GSR and eroded a precious stock of tyres and other spares.

A major change occurred on 1 January 1945 with the creation of Córas Iompair Éireann (CIÉ); this had been formed following the Transport Act of 1944 to take-over the assets of DUT and the Great Southern Railways Co. At the time, it was a statutory company; it was not nationalised until 1950 after the cessation of the last Dublin trams.

CIÉ inherited a network that included the five Dublin tram routes plus some 113 passenger trams and a policy that still anticipated the conversion of the surviving routes to bus operation. It was not, however, immediately possible for the new owners to complete the policy as other pressing needs required attention. Labour relations deteriorated with the result that there was a two-month strike – from 3 September to 2 November 1947 – that affected CIÉ's buses and trams.

However, by 1948, despite a certain amount of maintenance work being undertaken at Ballsbridge on the surviving tramcars, the arrival of new buses allowed for the process of tramway conversion to be resumed. The first of the routes to be replaced were routes 14 (Nelson Pillar to Dartry) and 15 (Nelson Pillar to Terenure); these were last operated on 31 October 1948. The final car from Nelson Pillar to Terenure was No 57, whilst the last to Dartry was No 291. Following this conversion, 13 four-wheel cars – Nos 6, 31, 129, 131, 132, 140, 154, 176, 193, 205, 246, 266 and 268 – were transferred to the Dalkey route to provide additional capacity.

The abandonment of routes 14 and 15 allowed for a slight revision in the terminal arrangements at Nelson Pillar for the Dalkey services to permit the elimination of some track and overhead. In early 1949, CIÉ ordered a second batch of double-deck buses; these were supplied by Leyland and were intended in part to permit the final conversion of the tramway. Although it was originally planned that the last trams would operate on 2 July 1949, problems meant a week's reprieve and the last services on the Dalkey route ran, therefore, on Saturday

9 July. Although a formal ceremony was planned, this was not carried out, with the result that the last service car, No 252, became de facto the city's last traditional tram. The last night was marred by some incidents of vandalism, with a number of the final trams – including No 252 – especially sustaining some damage.

Following closure, the surviving sixty-four passenger and works trams were mainly scrapped at Blackrock or Ballsbridge depots. Three trams – Nos 129/32 and 328 – were belatedly secured for preservation; unfortunately, stored in the open, the trio were subject to vandalism and were eventually scrapped. More recently the bodies of Nos 224/53/84 plus the unnumbered directors' saloon have been rescued. Nos 224/53 have been restored whilst the remaining two are under restoration.

DEPOTS
There were a considerable number of depots that served the trams operated by DUT. Ballsbridge depot and works, sited off Northumberland Road on Shelbourne Road, was opened by the Dublin Southern District Tramways in July 1879; it survived through to the system's final closure. Blackbanks depot was opened by the Clontarf & Hill of Howth Tramroad on 26 July 1900 and passed to DUT in 1908 with the operation of the line; it closed with the route on 29 March 1941. Blackrock depot on Newtown Avenue was originally a horse depot opened by the Blackrock & Kingstown Tramway Co in July 1879; the depot was extended in 1907 and survived until the withdrawal of the Dalkey services in July 1949. Clonksea was situated at the end of route 11; originally a horse tram depot opened by the Dublin Central Tramways in 1879, it closed with the route on 2 July 1939. Clontarf depot was located about a mile from the Dollymount terminus on Clontarf Road; it became a bus garage with the conversion of the Dollymount route on 31 May 1938 – the only tram depot so converted with

the exception of Conyngham Road – although five bogie cars allocated to the Howth service were housed initially at Conyngham Road and finally at Blackrock. Conyngham Road was inherited by DUT from the Dublin & Lucan following the take-over of the 3ft 0in line. Regauged to 5ft 2³⁄₁₆in, the depot survived until the closure of the services to Lucan on 12 April 1940. Dalkey depot, situated close to the terminus of the route, was opened by the Dublin Southern District Tramways in July 1879; it was to survive until the final demise of the system. Dartry depot opened with the route to Dartry on 27 January 1905 and also served route 12 to Palmerston Park; it was supplanted by Terenure in later years. Donnybrook was originally a horse depot opened by the Dublin Tramways Co and opened in early 1873; it closed with the withdrawal of services to Donnybrook on 2 June 1940. The permanent way sidings here remained in use until 1947. Inchicore, opened originally by the North Dublin Street Tramways Co, was the site of the main works as well as being a depot from 1907 and was renewed in 1936. It ceased to accommodate trams following withdrawal of the Inchicore service on 4 February 1940, work on tram maintenance already having ceased. Cabra depot, located on Phibsborough (North Circular Road), was opened by the North Dublin Street Tramways Co in 1876. Eventually housing trams for the Phoenix Park, Whitehall and Glasnevin services, it closed with the cessation of the last routes to Phoenix Park on 6 June 1940. Sandymount depot was situated on Gilford Road and was closed with the final conversion of the route serving Sandymount on 26 March 1940. A depot at Terenure was located on Rathfarnham Road and opened by the Dublin Central Tramways; this closed in 1908. The main depot here was situated on Terenure Road East was actually several separate sheds which were progressively joined together. This was also the site of a small horse tram works until replaced by Inchicore. Terenure depot was to survive through until the closure of the Terenure and Dartry routes in October 1948. Kingsbridge, on Victoria Quay, was located towards the terminus at Kingsbridge and was inherited from the Dublin Tramways Co; it closed in 1928 with its allocation transferred to Conyngham Road and the site sold to Guinness.

CLOSURES

31 October 1948	14 – Dartry;
	15 – Terenure
3 July 1949	6 – Blackrock; 7 – Dun Laoghaire; 8 – Dalkey

6, 8, 10/17, 44/46/49, 54, 60, 73, 87, 100/09/29/54/60/74/93/94/99, 209/15/43/46/59/79/87/91

Between 1922, when No 8 was built, and 1924, a total of thirty-three open-balcony cars were built at Inchcore on Brill 21E trucks. Between 1927 and 1930 all received new fully-enclosed top covers. These now matched the fifty-eight fully-enclosed 'Standard Saloons', which had been built between 1924 and 1929. These were again built at Inchcore on Brill 21E trucks. Of the 91 four-wheel cars, 63 were all withdrawn in 1940. These were Nos 2, 5, 7, 11, 14, 15, 20, 21, 24, 29, 36-38, 40, 47, 53, 58, 59, 67, 74, 90, 97, 106/11/14/16/18/21/24/25/27/ 30/36/44/46/58/62/68/70/71/89/92/96, 206/08/17/19/22/23/29/40/47/49/60/ 63-65/69/77/83/85/92/93. Of the surviving twenty-eight, nine had been those fitted with enclosed top covers; these were Nos 8 (enclosed top 1929), 44 (1928), 54 (1930), 100 (1930), 129 (1929), 160 (1927), 209 (1927), 279 (1929) and 291 (1929). All of the surviving cars were withdrawn in October 1948 with the exception of five – No 6, 129/54/93, 246 – that survived until the system's final demise in July 1949. No 129 was one of a trio of Dublin trams secured for preservation on closure, but was scrapped following vandalism.

Dublin No 17, seen here operating a route 15 service, was one of twenty-eight of the 'Standard Saloons' to survive post-war and was built originally in 1924. *F.N.T. Lloyd-Jones-Online Transport Archive*

9, 12/13, 22/23/6, 31/35, 41/43/45, 51/56/57, 78, 96, 102-04/23/31/32/35/38/40/48/53/67/76/96/97, 205/35/42/45/66/68

These thirty-seven 'Luxury Cars' were built at Spa Road works between 1931 and 1936; the quartet delivered in 1936 – Nos 102/03/67, 205 – were amongst the last new trams to be delivered to DUT. All were fitted with M&T swing-link four-wheel trucks with the exception of Nos 266/68, which were fitted with Brill 21E trucks. All of the batch survived to be taken over by CIÉ in 1945. Apart from nine cars – Nos 31, 131/32/38/40/76, 205/66/68 – transferred to the Dalkey line, all were withdrawn on 31 October 1948 following the conversion of the

Terenure and Dartry routes, although a number had not been in service for some time prior to this date. No 132 was the second of the three cars preserved at closure; it was also scrapped after sustaining vandalism.

70-72/79, 81-83, 112/13/17/85, 214/20/21/28/31, 328

These seventeen cars were the survivors of thirty-six open-balcony bogie cars supplied by Spa Road works between 1906 and 1924. All were fitted with Hurst Nelson bogies with the exception of Nos 313-15/18-23/25-30, which had M&G bogies. Some of the M&G-fitted cars were subsequently fitted with Hurst Nelson

'Luxury' No 131 was one of thirty-seven trams built between 1931 and 1936; it is pictured here at the Terenure terminus as the conductor turns the trolleypole. No 131 was one of nine of the batch to survive the closure of the Dartry and Terenure routes. *F. N. T. Lloyd-Jones/Online Transport Archive*

In all, seventeen balcony-top bogie cars survived the Second World War, including No 117 seen here on the Dun Laoghaire to Nelson Pillar route. *F.N.T. Lloyd-Jones /Online Transport Archive*

bogies. Of the remaining 19 cars, Nos 313 and 314 were built as fully enclosed in 1929 (see below) and four – Nos 326/27/29/30 – were rebuilt as fully enclosed 'Luxury' cars in 1934/36 (see below). The remaining thirteen cars – Nos 3, 64, 85, 91, 113, 313/15/18-22/25 – were all withdrawn between 1938 and 1944. Nos 320/21 were converted to single-deck in 1931 and 1932 and were subsequently both rebuilt as open-top double-deckers later in 1932. The original No 323 was renumbered 113 in 1944 on the withdrawal of the original No 113. The surviving cars were withdrawn following the conversion of the Dartry and Terenure routes in October 1948. No 328 was one of the trio of cars secured for

preservation on closure; unfortunately, being stored in the open, the car was subjected to vandalism and damage from the elements with the result that it was eventually scrapped.

93, 108/59/78, 273/80/82/94-300/16/17/26/27/29/30

Between 1931 and 1936, twenty 'Luxury' bogies cars were built or rebuilt at Spa Road Works on Hurst Nelson-built bogies; of these Nos 326/27/29/30 were rebuilds of earlier open-balcony cars, being completed in 1934 (Nos 329/30) and in 1936 (Nos 326/27). The last two to be completed – Nos 326/27 – differed slightly from the earlier eighteen, in seating

seventy-six (rather than seventy-four) and
having modified destination displays.
The first to be withdrawn was No 295 that
suffered fire damage and was scrapped
at Terenure in 1948. The remainder all
survived until the final closure of the
system in July 1949.

181/84, 218/24/52-55/78/84, 314
These eleven cars were 'Standard Saloons'
and were built at Spa Road works. Of
these, ten were built between 1925 and
1929, all were fitted with Hurst Nelson
bogies; No 314 was a rebuild of a bogie
open-balcony car and was completed
in 1929. There was a twelfth car of the

type – No 313 – but this was rebuilt from
the prototype 1906 car in 1929 and was
withdrawn in 1944. The first two – Nos
218/24 – were initially operated on the
Dalkey line but the subsequent nine were
built for use on the reopening of the Lucan
line in 1928. Following the conversion of
the Lucan route to bus operation in 1940,
the eleven cars were transferred to operate
over the Dalkey route. All survived until
the conversion of the Dalkey route in July
1949 and were subsequently scrapped.
However, although not preserved at
the time, the bodies of two of the type –
Nos 253 and 284 – have been subsequently
salvaged.

Recorded outside
Blackrock depot,
No 280 was one
of twenty 'Luxury'
bogie cars in service
after the war. All,
bar No 295, survived
until the system's
final closure.
*F.N.T. Lloyd-Jones /
Online Transport
Archive (FNTLJ-194)*

No 314 was one of eleven 'Standard Saloon' bogie cars to survive into 1945; it is seen here at the Dalkey terminus of route 8 prior to heading back to Nelson Pillar. *Barry Cross Collection/ Online Transport Archive*

DIRECTORS' CAR

Constructed at Spa Road works – the 203rd tram to be completed there – the Directors' Car was completed in June 1901. Never allocated a fleet number the car was initially fitted with a Peckham truck, but this was replaced by one manufactured at Spa Road in 1909. Lavishly fitted out, with twelve armchairs on the lower deck, for example, the car was to survive through until the final closure of the system in July 1949, although it was effectively withdrawn in the late 1930s. Following the conversion, the car was purchased privately by Mr H. Porter in 1950. In the late twentieth century, whilst negotiations were in hand to effect its sales to Irish National Tramway Museum, the body suffered severe fire damage as the result of vandalism. Much of the vehicle, however,

survives and it is hoped that it will eventually be restored.

WORKS CARS

Dublin had a large and varied fleet of works cars but the majority of these had been withdrawn before the takeover by CIÉ. Apart from the Directors' Car, there were five other survivors. These were water car No 4, haulage wagon No 24, engineering car No 31, stores wagon No 51 and grinder No 73. No 4 was fitted with a Brill truck and scrapped in 1949. No 24 dated originally from *circa* 1910 and, based at Ballsbridge, was to survive until 1949. No 31 was one of the Milnes-built cars delivered between 1896 and 1898. Fitted with a Peckham truck, it was cut down for works duties in the 1930s and was withdrawn when the permanent way yard

The unnumbered DUT Directors' Car was built at Spa Road in 1901 and was to survive – albeit largely out of use from the late 1930s – through until final closure. *Barry Cross Collection/Online Transport Archive*

at Donnybrook closed in 1947. No 51 was converted in 1933 from 1900-built open-top car No 203, which had been originally built by Browne in 1900. No 51 was withdrawn in 1948. Finally, No 73 was a further conversion from one of the Milnes-built cars of 1896-98. It survived until the end of the system.

The history of Dublin's works fleet is complex but the majority had been withdrawn before CIÉ acquired DUT. One of the survivors was No 73; this was a railgrinder that had been converted from one of the late nineteenth century Milnes-built cars. *Phil Tatt/Online Transport Archive*

FINTONA

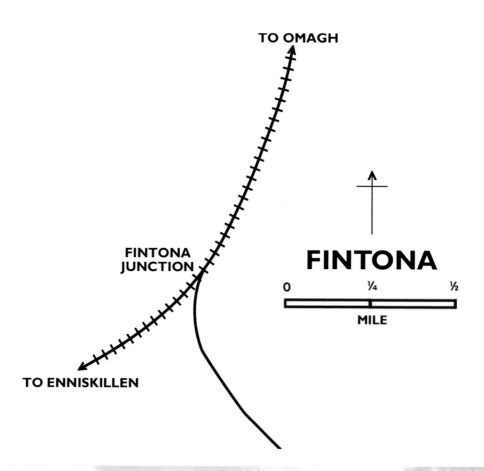

TO OMAGH

FINTONA JUNCTION

TO ENNISKILLEN

FINTONA

0   ¼   ½

MILE

On 10 June 1957, towards the end of the line's life, the single horse tram used on the Fintona branch is pictured at the line's terminus. *Paul de Beer/Online Transport Archive*

The slightly anachronistic operation of a horse tramway between Fintona Junction and Fintona survived through the war and the 1940s largely unchanged but the parlous start of the railway's finances were to worsen as the decade wore on.

The line – 5ft 3in in gauge and ½-mile in length – ran south from Fintona Junction, on the GNR(I) Enniskillen to Omagh line. The passenger traffic was handled by a horse tram hauled by a single horse – and always reputedly called Dick irrespective of gender – whilst all freight traffic was handled by steam. The lack of a spare tram was not to be a major problem except briefly in 1953. On 17 January, the tram was seriously damaged when the then Dick bolted; although the tram remained in service for a short period, it had to be sent to Dundalk for repair. Whilst No 381 was away, passengers' luggage was conveyed in the tram's open trailer whilst passengers had to make the journey on foot.

In some respects, the accident was a portent of the future as the financial condition of the GNR(I) worsened. The company had been excluded from the creation of the nationalised Ulster Transport Authority in Northern Ireland and from Córas Iompair Éireann, which was nationalised in 1950, in the Republic. Following the GNR(I)'s failure, ownership was transferred on 1 September 1953 to a new body – the Great Northern Railway Board – which was jointly controlled by the governments in Belfast and Dublin. This was never a happy arrangement,

The Fintona horse tram No 381 pictured alongside the platform at Fintona Junction with the Enniskillen to Omagh main line in the background. *W.A. Camwell/National Tramway Museum*

particularly as the former was antipathetic towards its railway network. The situation deteriorated in 1956 when the Northern Minister of Commerce announced unilaterally the closure of 115 miles of the former GNR(I) network in Ulster.

These plans, which included the closure of the Enniskillen to Omagh line as well as the Fintona branch, were rejected by the Dublin government and were, therefore, submitted to the Transport Tribunals in Belfast and Dublin; the former accepted the closures, the latter rejected them. As a result, on 5 July 1957, the Northern Minister of Commerce announced that the routes would close three months later on 30 September.

The closures went ahead as planned; following the withdrawal of the Fintona branch service, No 381 was preserved.

DEPOT

The Fintona branch did not possess a depot as such, although Fintona station did have a short overall roof. There was a shed at Fintona Junction where the horse was stabled. The horses employed on the line were often alarmed by steam engines and so usually had to be kept in the shed whilst main line trains steamed through Fintona Junction.

CLOSURES

30 September 1957   Fintona Junction to Fintona Town

FLEET

381

In 1877, it was decided that the existing horse tram needed replacement; however, it was not until 1883 that the new tram was delivered from the Metropolitan Railway Carriage & Wagon Co of Birmingham. The new four-wheel tram was originally delivered as No 74 and finished in varnished mahogany; it was subsequently renumbered 381, in the GNR(I)'s carriage sequence, and repainted in blue and cream. In order to supplement this one vehicle, a second tram, No 416, was constructed at Dundalk in 1913, but this was destroyed by fire before it could be sent to Fintona. No 381 accommodated three classes of passenger; the enclosed lower deck housed first- and second-class passengers in two separate sections whilst third-class occupied the open top-deck. No 381 was to remain at Fintona until the closure of the line on 30 September 1957. On withdrawal, No 381 and its trailer were preserved and is now on display in the Ulster Folk & Transport Museum.

No 381 was constructed by the GNR(I) in 1883; it had a wheelbase of 10ft 0in and an overall length of 25ft 0in – considerably larger than most urban horse trams – and offered a seating capacity of forty-eight. It is seen here at Fintona Junction. *Marcus Eavis/Online Transport Archive*

GIANT'S CAUSEWAY

GIANTS CAUSEWAY

0 ¼ ½ ¾ 1
MILE

GIANTS CAUSEWAY

VICTORIA BRIDGE

BUSHMILLS

PORTRUSH

On 21 September 1948, towards the end of that year's summer season, No 21 is recorded with a trailer at Bushmills. No 21 was one of the power cars that was fitted with glazed windscreens for operation during the winter months. *Ian L. Wright/Online Transport Archive*

On the same day, the much modified No 9 is seen at the Giant's Causeway terminus. This is the only power car from the line to survive; it is currently undergoing restoration at Howth. *Ian L. Wright/ Online Transport Archive*

Having survived into 1945 and the worst effects of the war, the Giant's Causeway faced a new challenge in January 1945 when, following a heavy snowfall on the 20th, services were suspended for ten days as a result of snowdrifts and a frozen turbine at Bushmills.

One of the consequences of the war and the stationing of troops in the area had been the reintroduction of a winter service in 1940 – prior to that services had ended at the end of the summer season for a number of years. As the war progressed, the necessity of operating a winter service had resulted in modifications to a number of cars; this included the fitting of glazed ends to Nos 20 and 23 in 1943; this process continued during the winter of 1945/46 with glazed ends being fitted to No 21 but planned work on No 22 was not carried out the following

winter as a result of other necessary maintenance work and the end of the war. Other work on the fleet in 1945 included the rebuilding of No 9, which emerged in its new guise in June. Also during 1945, the overhead was extended to the one road at the Portrush depot that had previously only been accessible by flyshunting.

Although the military requirement was much reduced, a winter service was once again operated over 1945/46. The new year saw the generator at Walkmills given an overhaul and the main dam there repaired. Considerable maintenance work was undertaken during the winter of 1946/47 although a winter service was again maintained. In July 1947, fares were increased. The low level of the River Bush resulted in the necessity of using the diesel generator between mid-August and 6 September 1947. The fleet of the threatened Bessbrook & Newry was investigated with a view to possible purchase; however, the trams were deemed unsuitable and no acquisitions resulted.

In September 1947, it was decided to retain the winter service despite the low returns achieved over the winter of 1946/47. However, the returns were again poor and on 27 December 1947 it was agreed to suspend services until Easter 1948.

In early January 1948, the Ulster Transport Authority was created; in June that year it was suggested at a board meeting of the Giant's Causeway that the tramway be offered to the new undertaking as new ownership would absolve the company of any liability for road restoration in the event of the tramway's closure. The UTA, however, declined the offer three months later.

In September 1948, the line's engineer resigned; both he and his replacement were pessimistic about the physical condition of the track and structures. As a result, a considerable amount of work – track relaying and the replacement of the timber decking on the Jubilee Bridge, for example – was undertaken in late 1948 and early 1949. Following the suspension of the winter service in December 1947, it was agreed that there would be no winter service in 1948/49 and so services ended for the year on 30 September.

Although the work undertaken on the line suggested that it might have a future, in reality these hopes were dashed. As in 1948, services ceased for the year in 1949 on 30 September at the end of the summer season; although not known at the time, the Giant's Causeway Tramway had operated for the last time. In November 1949, when the manager reported the poor financial results for the summer season, the board decided to wind up the company (in reality not a straightforward procedure). A public announcement to this effect was made in November 1949 and led to an immediate public outcry. Efforts

were made to try and save the line but at a Board meeting in August 1950 it was estimated that it would cost £15,000 to see services reinstated. On 22 September 1950, interested bodies met the Northern Ireland government to seek support but this was not forthcoming. As a result, the company sought an abandonment order; this, as a result of opposition, was not made effective until September 1951 but, by that date, the line's demise had been confirmed by a sale in Belfast on 31 March 1951 of the company's track, vehicles and assets.

Three of the company's fleet were eventually to be preserved – Nos 2, 5 and 9 – whilst, in 2002, a two-mile section of the line from Bushmills to Giant's Causeway reopened as a 3ft 0in gauge steam railway.

DEPOT

The Giant's Causeway Tramway was served throughout its life by two depots; these was located at Portrush and at Bushmills. At Portrush there were two primary buildings: one housed the electric tramcars and a second provided a shed for the line's steam locomotives whilst a single shed served the latter. Both opened with the line and survived through to the line's closure on 30 September 1949.

CLOSURES

30 September 1949	Giant's Causeway to Portrush

FLEET

Due to the lack of detailed records the fleet history of the Giant's Causeway Tramway cannot be precise, but the following were in service when the line ceased operation on 30 September 1949. Whilst a number of vehicles were originally delivered to accommodate either first- or third-class passengers, the former was abandoned in 1923 and all cars thereafter accommodated single-class passengers. All were disposed of after closure. The company's four steam locomotives, all built by Wilkinson of Wigan were disposed of as follows: No 1 was converted into a ballast wagon in 1910;

No 2 was scrapped in 1899; Nos 3 *Dunluce Castle* and 4 *Brian Boroihme* were sold in 1930 to a contractor involved engaged in work on the River Bann Navigation near Portstewart.

1/2

For the opening of the line the Midland Railway Carriage & Wagon Co supplied two closed first-class trailers; these were Nos 1 and 2. Both survived to the line's closure and No 2 is now preserved in a fully restored condition at Cultra.

3/4

Two first-class power cars, Nos 3 and 4, were also built by the Midland Railway Carriage & Wagon Co. Although originally fitted with motors, both were converted to unpowered trailers by 1902 and were to survive in this guise through to 1945 but, during that year, No 3, which had not been used for a number of years, was dismantled with its body panels being used for rebuilding No 9.

5-7

Three open third-class six-bench trailer cars were also delivered for the line's opening by the Midland Railway Carriage & Wagon Co. These trailers could accommodate twenty-four passengers. Following closure, No 5 was preserved and is now on display at Cultra.

9

The original delivery date and nature of No 9 are uncertain, but is seems likely to have been delivered in about 1889, although recent restoration work has suggested an earlier date. No 9 was unusual in that it was split between first and third-class accommodation, with a sliding door separating the two sections. In 1909, No 9 was converted into a power car following the acquisition of a further Peckham truck. This required work to accommodate the trolleypole as its original body was not designed to support such equipment. The body was further modified to improve the protection for the crew

For the line's opening two trailer cars – Nos 1 and 2 – were supplied by the Midland Railway Carriage & Wagon Co. The latter, later preserved, is recorded here at the head of a three-car set. *C. Carter*

One of the three trailers supplied by the Midland Railway Carriage & Wagon Co, No 6, stands at Portrush on 7 June 1948. *John Meredith/ Online Transport Archive*

Giant's Causeway No 9 is pictured at Portrush on 7 June 1948; this is after the car was modified through the use of the ornate side panels recovered when No 3 was dismantled. *John Meredith/Online Transport Archive*

on the platforms shortly afterwards. In 1945 the body of No 9 was refurbished through the use of the ornate side panels from No 3. Eventually, after a long period of storage as a café in Youghal, Co Cork No 9 was secured for preservation; it is currently under restoration at Howth.

10

Closed saloon trailer No 10 is also of uncertain provenance but again seems to have been delivered in about 1889. From No 10 onwards, all the toast-rack cars supplied were open on one side only.

11/13/15/16

In 1888 five goods wagons were converted into small five-bench trailers; these were Nos 11-15. A further two, Nos 16 and 17, were converted three years later. Four of the type survived through to September 1949.

19

In 1897, two further crossbench toast-rack trailers were acquired – Nos 18 and 19. These provided accommodation for twenty-eight passengers. Only one of the duo, No 19, survived through to final closure.

20/21

In July 1899, for the inauguration of the overhead system, two single-deck open toast-rack trams were acquired – Nos 20 and 21; these were fitted with Peckham Cantilever trucks.

22

In 1902 a further seven-bench toast-rack power car, No 22, was delivered; this was fitted with a Peckham truck.

23

A further seven-bench toast-rack power car, No 23, was delivered in 1908; this was, however, fitted with a UEC Patent suspension Truck.

24

No 24 was the last tram to enter service with the Giant's Causeway Tramway. In 1937 two 3ft 6in gauge double-deck trams were acquired from Dunfermline & District. Whilst one was not used, No 37 – which dated originally to 1917 and was built by UEC being fitted with a UEC-built Peckham P22 truck – was cut down to single-deck and regauged for use in Ireland.

Giant's Causeway closed trailer saloon No 10 seen attached to the refurbished No 9. *Desmond Coakham*

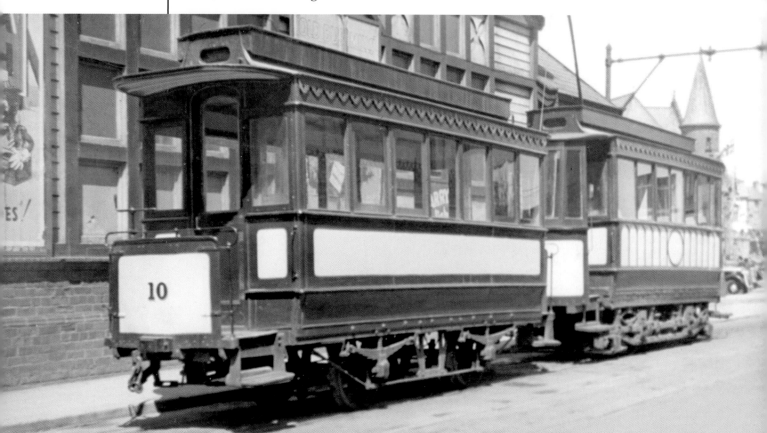

One of the converted goods wagons, No 11, stands at Portrush in a set that also includes two other trailers, No 5 and 6. *John Meredith/Online Transport Archive*

One of the two trams acquired in 1899, No 20, recorded on 27 July 1948. *Tony Wickens/Online Transport Archive*

The last tram to enter service on the Giant's Causeway line was No 24; this had originally been a Dunfermline & District double-deck car but was modified before operation in Ireland. It is seen at Giant's Causeway on 7 June 1948. *John Meredith/Online Transport Archive*

Giant's Causeway No 23, built originally in 1908, stands at the terminus at Giants Causeway with two trailer cars. *Martin Jenkins Collection/ Online Transport Archive*

GREAT ORME

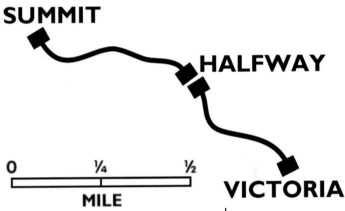

GREAT ORME

SUMMIT

HALFWAY

VICTORIA

0   ¼   ½

MILE

In July 1972 No 5 is pictured at the terminus of the lower section of the Great Orme Tramway in Llandudno. *W. J. Wyse/LRTA (London Area) Collection/Online Transport Archive*

Given its problems of the previous decade, the survival of the Great Orme Tramway into the post-war years was almost miraculous; survive it did but its ownership was soon to change.

Under the 1898 Act that permitted the construction of the line, Llandudno Corporation had powers to purchase the line. In 1947, the corporation decided to exercise this option although there was a considerable disagreement over the actual price. This resulted in the corporation

exercising powers of compulsory purchase in November 1948, backdated to 31 March 1948, with the effective date of the transfer of ownership being 1 January 1949. With its prime asset now in corporation ownership, Great Orme Railway Ltd was formally wound up in 1950.

Under corporation ownership there were some changes. In 1949, a second overhead wire was added to the upper section. In 1956, following an estimation that conversion to electric operation would save £1,400 per annum, a contract was

Shortly after the corporation take-over of the line, No 6 is seen at Halfway with the depot and engine house in the background. The date is 2 July 1950 and the steam engine is still in use; later in the decade steam power would be replaced by electricity. *John Meredith/Online Transport Archive*

On 5 July 1972, Great Orme No 5 descends towards the lower-section terminus. The tram is carrying the royal blue livery adopted in 1967 with its side panels proclaiming, 'Great Orme Railway'. *W. J. Wyse/ LRTA (London Area) Collection/Online Transport Archive*

signed with English Electric to replace the steam-driven winding gear at Halfway; 1957 was to witness the last operation of the steam-driven equipment. In 1965, a brick-built passenger shelter was added at Halfway

In 1962, a new bright blue livery was adopted; this was to last until 1967, when royal blue was adopted and this to 1977, when Trafalgar blue appeared. The latter year also saw the line revert to its original title, with 'Tramway' replacing 'Railway' on the side of the vehicles. By this date, two further changes of ownership had taken place, when, following local government reorganisation, Aberconwy County Council assumed responsibility in April 1974; control passed the Conwy County Borough Council in 1977.

By the late 1980s, financial pressures on the local authority resulted in rumours that the council was looking to dispose of the tramway and, for a period, it was suggested that Bolton Tramways Ltd, the group behind the restoration of Bolton No 66, might take over. In the event, operation was transferred to the Direct Services Department of the council in 1990. The new operators acted to reverse a period of lack of maintenance with track being relaid and the introduction of new radio communication equipment. The latter permitted the removal of the overhead on both sections; this had only ever been installed for communication purposes and was now redundant. It was expected that some sections of the overhead would be restored for cosmetic purposes but this has not been undertaken. In 1991, operation of the tram changed to one-man control with dead-man (vigilance) control.

The summer of 1992 witnessed some changes. On 31 July, a new summit station was formally opened whilst there was a further livery change with an ornate blue and gold scheme adopted. Plans for a viewing platform and new shelter at Halfway were also announced. To mark the 90th anniversary of the opening of the lower section, special anniversary tickets were issued on 31 July and 1/2 August, when services also ran for longer than usual.

Services the following year were disrupted for three weeks in the summer when, following a cloudburst on 10 June

No 4 is seen outside the rebuilt station at Halfway; the refurbishment programme saw the reconstruction of the depots and winding house at Halfway to provide a modern interchange facility. *P. Bannister/Online Transport Archive*

1993, ballast on the upper section was partially lost and mud blocked the conduit on the lower section. Following repairs, the line reopened on 2 July, although the loss of traffic was estimated to have cost the line £30,000 in lost revenue.

By the end of the decade, the physical condition of the line was starting to give concern and a major project of refurbishment, part funded by the European Union and the Heritage Lottery Fund, was instituted in 1999; this was ultimately to cost some £4.5 million and take a number of years to complete. Prior to this work being undertaken, some £140,000 was spent on major track renewals on the lower section. During the summer of 1999, damage was caused to a number of properties alongside the lower section when one of the redundant trolleypoles swung loose from a moving tram whilst, for about a week leading up

to 30 July the same year, the tramway was closed in order to facilitate the removal by specialist contractors of some asbestos.

Following on from the fatal accident in 1932, the tramway had almost seventy years without a serious incident; however, on 30 April 2000, Nos 6 and 7 collided head on, resulting in thirty-seven passengers being injured of whom seventeen required hospital treatment. The initial problem was believed to be a faulty point although the accident report indicated that there was also a problem of staff training. The collision resulted in the temporary suspension of services and the replacement of the suspect point. A second – less serious – collision occurred at the same loop on 15 September 2009; on this occasion, wear on the rails and point mechanism was identified as the cause.

The most significant part of the refurbishment programme affected

The two lower section cars – Nos 4 and 5 – pass at the intermediate loop on Ty-Gwyn Road, Llandudno. No 4 was the car seriously damaged in the 1932 accident that almost resulted in the line's closure. *Phil Tatt/ Online Transport Archive*

Halfway. Here, the work involved the demolition of the original two sheds and their replacement by a single structure that would also accommodate the winding room for the cables and act as an interchange space for passengers passing between the upper and lower sections. Although there were delays to the overall programme of works, partly as a result of the number of utility pipes and cables encountered along with poor weather when upgrading the lower section track during 2004, the complete project was completed in time for the line's reopening for the 2005 season.

The tramway celebrated its centenary in 2002 and its 110th anniversary a decade later; the line today remains a popular part of Llandudno's heritage, carrying some 160,000 passengers annually.

DEPOTS

As a form of funicular and with two distinct sections, there are four buildings serving the Great Orme tramway, each capable of accommodating a single car. There is Victoria station (in Llandudno), two at Halfway and one at the Summit. All were opened with the line in 1904 and all remain operational although the structures at Halfway were heavily rebuilt following the refurbishment programme from 1999 onwards that resulted in the new Halfway station.

FLEET

4/5

The two cars for use on the lower section were both manufactured by Hurst Nelson and were delivered in 1902 for the opening of the line. Both cars remain in service.

6/7

Hurst Nelson was also to supply the two cars for the upper section; these were delivered in 1903. Again, both remain in service.

The driver controls upper-section No 7 as it departs from the summit. The overhead and trolleypoles are shown to good effect; these were required for communication rather than to transmit power. *Phil Tatt/Online Transport Archive*

HILL OF HOWTH

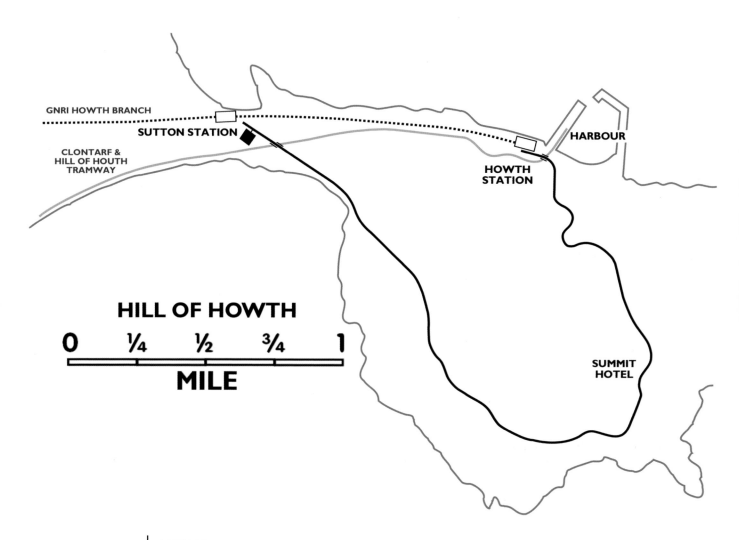

GNRI HOWTH BRANCH

SUTTON STATION

CLONTARF &
HILL OF HOUTH
TRAMWAY

HARBOUR

HOWTH
STATION

HILL OF HOWTH

0   ¼   ½   ¾   1

MILE

SUMMIT
HOTEL

The Hill of Howth tramway entered the Second World War still as a subsidiary of the Great Northern Railway (I) but its future had been under discussion prior to the start of the war. Between the two world wars, the tramway had been subject to six reports into its future; initially thoughts of replacing the tramway with buses had foundered on the grounds that the gradients of the route (up to 1 in 8½) were unsuitable for the buses of the day and, by the 1930s, although bus technology had improved, the finances of the GNR(I) had deteriorated significantly.

The wartime years led to an improvement – albeit temporary – in the financial position of the GNR(I) but, like DUT, services on the Hill of Howth tramway were suspended between

With the CIÉ station in the background, Hill of Howth No 6 stands at Howth. *Phil Tatt/Online Transport Archive*

June and September 1944 as a result of the acute hydro electric shortage that Ireland was suffering at the time. For the summer of 1944, therefore, buses operated in place of the trams – a portent of the future. The trams resumed running as soon as the power was restored on 25 September 1944.

Although the railways of Ireland had, in the main, been transferred to the nationalised Ulster Transport Authority in Northern Ireland and to Córas Iompair Éireann, which was nationalised in 1950, in Ireland, the GNR(I) retained its independence. However, by the early 1950s, the company's financial position worsened considerably, despite its best endeavours to reduce costs – through the development of multiple-unit operation,

for example – and on 1 September 1953 it was taken over by the two governments and reconstituted as the Great Northern Railway Board.

Each government nominated five members to the new board and the priority was to improve the railway's finances. On 28 January 1954, one of the first actions of the new board was to announce the closure of the Hill of Howth tramway on 31 March 1954. This led to a storm of protests but, once again, the condition of the roads locally saved the line at least temporarily. Due to their poor state, the Irish government's Department of Industry and Commerce agreed to underwrite the losses for at least two years whilst the roads were improved.

Two of the original Hill of Howth cars – Nos 4 and 8 – meet at the Summit. *Phil Tatt/Online Transport Archive*

This work was completed and, in early 1957, the first trials using replacement buses were operated. During 1957, following examination of the fleet, two of the original cars – Nos 5 and 8 – were withdrawn and cannibalised for spare parts. The remains of these two did, however, survive until the system's final closure.

The tramway's ownership changed again in 1958; during 1957, much of the board's railway network had been closed and a threat remained to much of that which survived. On 30 September 1958, at the end of the five-year agreement that set the board up, it was dissolved with the assets in the Republic passing to CIÉ on the following day. The loss-making Hill of Howth was an easy target for an administration keen to reduce losses and, although there were efforts to dissuade CIÉ from the action, on 14 May 1959 it was announced that the line was to close on 31 May 1959.

The last day witnessed vast crowds with all eight of the serviceable passenger trams in operation. The last tram to operate was No 9; its final passage, however, was curtailed as a red signal indicated a missing fishplate near Stella Maris. The cause of this loss is uncertain but was most likely an act of vandalism as the line had suffered some lesser problems during this final day.

With the passenger service now ended, work commenced rapidly on the line's demolition using, initially, the sole works car (No 11). The first track was lifted in November 1959 and the work was completed in January 1960.

DEPOT

The Hill of Howth tramway was served by a single depot that was located at the Sutton end of the line. It opened with the tramway in 1901 and was to survive through until closure on 31 May 1959.

CLOSURE

31 May 1959   Sutton station to Howth station

1-8

To open the line, Brush supplied eight open-top double-deck trams fitted with Brill 22E maximum traction bogies. These trams had a seating capacity of sixty-seven and were fitted with windscreens but with the offside of each vestibule left open originally, but this was later enclosed. All eight were to survive until the end of the line in 1959 although Nos 5 and 8 had been withdrawn and cannibalised for spares in 1957. Three of the cars were initially secured for preservation: No 2 want to California, where it is now displayed at the Orange Empire Trolley Museum; No 4 is at present housed at the Ulster Folk & Transport Museum at Cultra; and, No 3 was originally saved for display locally. However, it, along with Nos 9 and 11, was left in the open and suffered from vandalism and it was eventually scrapped.

9/10

In 1902, two additional summer only cars were supplied, but by Milnes instead. Again open-top, the two cars were larger than the original eight, seating seventy-three, and were fitted with Peckham 14D5 maximum traction bogies. When delivered, the lower-deck windows were fitted with wire mesh rather than being glazed but this was soon changed. Both cars survived to the end although they tended to be less heavily used until 1958 (when modified with cross-springs reused from Nos 5 and 8) than the original eight; both were preserved in 1959. No 10 passed to the Tramway Museum Society in Britain; regauged to 4ft 8½in the car has seen service in Blackpool. At the time of writing it is on display at the National Tramway Museum at Crich. Like No 3, No 9 was originally bought for preservation locally; unlike No 3, however, despite the ravages of time and vandalism, the remains of No 9 were rescued and, with its body fully restored, No 9 now forms part of the collection of the National Transport Museum of Ireland.

One of the eight original cars, No 4, stands outside Sutton depot. At this date, the original trams were in a livery of blue and cream; this colour scheme dated originally to the 1930s. Originally, the trams had been painted crimson lake and ivory. *R.W.A. Jones/Online Transport Archive*

Two additional passenger cars – Nos 9 and 10 – were acquired in 1902. The former is pictured here in the grained mahogany livery adopted for the entire fleet about 1912. Nos 9 and 10 were the only cars not to receive the later blue and white livery. *R.W.A. Jones/Online Transport Archive*

11

Believed to have been constructed at Dundalk in 1903, No 11 was a goods car initially and afterwards it became the line's works car. When built, it lacked dedicated running gear, being fitted with such equipment as and when required from one of the passenger fleet. No 11 was eventually fitted with Brill 22E maximum traction bogies. As with the passenger fleet, No 11 survived until the line's closure and, with Nos 3 and 9, was acquired for preservation locally. Unfortunately, suffering from vandalism, the remains of No 11 were eventually scrapped.

The Hill of Howth possessed one dedicated works car – No 11. It is seen here outside Sutton depot on 8 August 1955. *Tony Wickens/ Online Transport Archive*

LLANDUDNO & COLWYN BAY

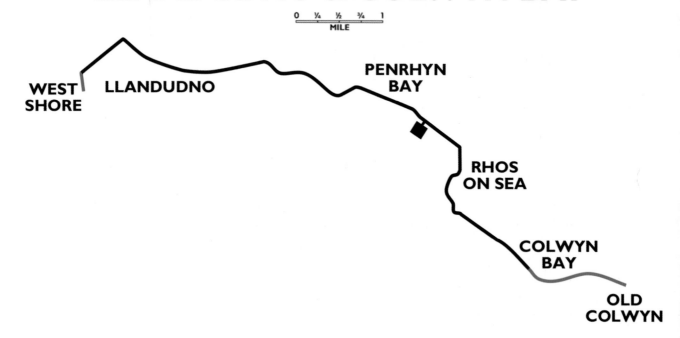

LLANDUDNO & COLWYN BAY

0   ¼   ½   ¾   1
MILE

WEST SHORE

LLANDUDNO

PENRHYN BAY

RHOS ON SEA

COLWYN BAY

OLD COLWYN

The Llandudno & Colwyn Bay Electric Railway had entered the war in a reasonably good condition. During 1938, the line's overhead had been completely replaced whilst much of the fleet had been renewed during the 1930s through the acquisition of second-hand trams from Bournemouth and Accrington. These vehicles saw the company operate double-deck trams for the first time. The company also benefited during the war from increased traffic with a number of government departments transferred to the area.

Towards the end of 1945, two events occurred that were less positive, however. In October, the sea wall at Penrhyn Bay was washed away, severely damaging the seaward track. This was not the first occasion when sea damage had occurred here – similar events had occurred in 1927, 1933 and 1943 – but was the most serious to date. Such was the damage that single-line operation was necessary for two weeks whilst repairs were completed. The following month saw No 16, one of the three surviving cars from 1907, severely damaged by fire; it was subsequently scrapped.

In 1946, the company added to its fleet through the purchase of the two streamlined cars supplied originally to Darwen Corporation in 1936. Following conversion to 3ft 6in, the two cars were

One of the ex-Bournemouth cars, No 11, heads around Palladium Corner in Llandudno heading towards the West Shore terminus. During busy periods, many cars from Colwyn Bay terminated here. *Phil Tatt/Online Transport Archive*

Part of the street section through Colwyn Bay was provided with interlaced track; here one of the quartet of toast-rack cars supplied in 1920, No 20, heads west from the Colwyn Bay terminus over this section. *Phil Tatt/Online Transport Archive*

The damage caused by the sea at Penryhn Bay over the winter of 1952/53 is all too evident in this view of ex-Bournemouth No 8. The costs of restoration were such that the line was singled. *Phil Tatt/Online Transport Archive*

It is last evening of the Llandudno & Colwyn Bay Electric Railway and No 4 is packed with passengers eager to take a last journey over the line. *F.E.J. Ward Online Transport Archive*

officially tested by the Ministry of Transport on 14 April 1948. The results of the tests were a disappointment as the Ministry banned their operation over the section from Bodafan Fields through to the depot at Rhos in public service. As a result, the two trams were limited to operating shuttles between West Shore and Nant-y-Gamar Road in Llandudno and between the depot and Colwyn Bay.

In addition to the purchase of Nos 23 and 24, the company also undertook work on the line's infrastructure. During 1946 and 1947, the section of track between Colwyn Crescent and Church Road was relaid. This was followed in November 1952 by the relaying of track in Mostyn Street whilst further work, including the relocation of a crossover in Colwyn bay, was completed in 1953 and 1954. The most significant event was, however, less positive. The track at Penrhyn Bay had again been undermined during the winter of 1948/49; repair work again required the use of temporary single-track working. In 1952/53 the same happened; however, the cost of repairing the track was complicated by a grant from the government to the local authority for the construction of improved sea defences – which the company believed might deprive it of the tolls from the company-owned toll road that supplemented its revenue from the trams – with the result that the line was singled for the remainder of the tramway's life. The work included repoling the section with second-hand traction columns acquired from Stockport.

The decision not to restore the double track at Penrhyn Bay was evidence of the deteriorating financial position of the tramway. In 1953 the company's results had shown a loss of £1,122 but this had risen to £3,004 the following year as a result of a decline of some 47,000 passengers to 2,698,000 (and despite an increase in fares on 5 July 1953). By the early 1950s, the railway preservation movement had started and the perceived threat to the tramway saw efforts made to try and save the line with several appeals made through the pages of *Modern Tramway* and attempts to try and purchase shares in the company.

Whilst these efforts were going on, the company acquired its first bus, an ex-East Kent Leyland Titan TD5, in September 1955 for crew-training purposes. On 14 September 1955 came the news that the enthusiast fraternity had dreaded: the formal announcement that the line was to close. Two factors (both ultimately solved), however, meant that the closure could not take place immediately. The first issue was that, on 12 October 1955, the Traffic Commissioners for the North West Area stated that the closure could not go ahead until a joint timetable had been agreed between Crosville and the tramway. The second issue was the cost liability in reinstating the roads once the tramway closed.

The tramway's fate was, however, sealed as a result of action by the Manchester & North Western Electricity Board. The Board, faced by a number of small local and uneconomic generating stations, estimated that eight men were employed solely for the purposes of generating power for the tramway. It, therefore, gave notice that after the existing contract to supply power expired – in the summer of 1956 – it would only continue to supply power at the prohibitive rate of £100 per day. This forced the tramway board's hand and a decision was made to cease operation. The last trams operated on 24 March 1956 with ex-Bournemouth car No 8 acting as the official last car. The company had acquired additional buses quickly to permit the conversion; six were available at closure.

Following closure, the majority of trams were dismantled at Rhos depot, although ex-Bournemouth No 6 was secured for preservation. The Llandudno & Colwyn Bay Co continued to operate buses for five years, until it sold out to long-tern rival, Crosville.

DEPOT

The Llandudno & District Electric Traction Co Ltd opened its only depot – the eight-road shed at Tramway Road, Rhos-on-Sea – on 19 October 1907. This was the home of the tramway fleet right through until final closure on of the system on 24 March 1956.

CLOSURE
24 March 1956   West Shore to Colwyn Bay

1-5
In 1932, L&CBER acquired five ex-Accrington Corporation single-deck trams. Originally, Accrington Nos 28-32 respectively, the quintet were built in 1915 (Nos 28-30) and 1921 (Nos 31/32) by Brush. When sold to L&CBER, Nos 2 and 5 retained their original Brush-built maximum traction bogies but regauged from 4ft 0in to 3ft 6in whilst Nos 1, 3 and 4 received M&G equal-wheel bogies from the original L&CBER fleet. All were withdrawn for scrap in 1956.

6-15
In 1936, a further batch of second-hand trams was acquired, this time ten open-top double-deck cars that had previously operated in Bournemouth. The cars were originally Bournemouth Nos 85 (of 1914), 115/16, 108/03, 95, 128/12/21/14 respectively. Bournemouth Nos 114-6/21 were new in 1925/26, Nos 95, 103, 108 and 112 were new in 1921 and No 128 in 1927. All were fitted with Brush bodies with the exception of No 6 which was built by UEC. All survived until withdrawal in 1955/56. No 6 was preserved as part of the National Collection; it was restored as Bournemouth No 85 and is now on display in Crich. The Llandudno & Colwyn Bay Tramway Society has restored the body of Bournemouth No 126 as L&CBER No 7, although No 126 never actually operated on the line.

One of five ex-Accrington single-deck cars, No 2, stands outside the depot at Rhos-on-Sea. This had originally been Accrington No 32 and dated to 1921. No 2 retained its original Brush-built maximum traction bogies regauged to 3ft 6in. *R. W. A. Jones/Online Transport Archive*

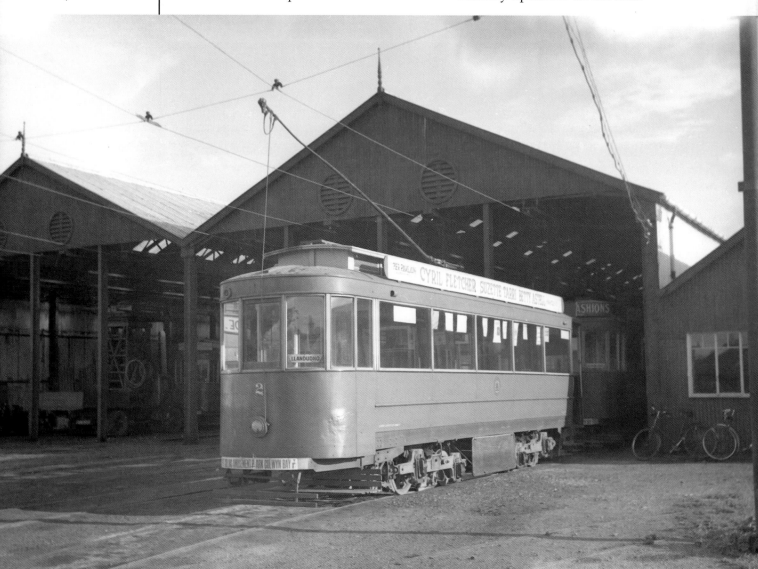

16-18
This trio of trams represented the last of the L&CBER's original fleet to remain in service. These were originally Nos 6, 14 and 11 respectively and were renumbered in the early 1930s. They were built by the Midland Railway Carriage & Wagon Co on M&G equal-wheel bogies. No 16 was withdrawn in late 1945 following fire damage whilst No 18 probably last appeared in 1954. No 17 suffered accident damage just before the system closed. Both were scrapped after closure.

19-22
In 1920, L&CBER acquired a batch of four open single-deck toast-rack cars from English Electric. These were fitted with English Electric-built bogies and could accommodate sixty seated passengers. The quartet was last operated during the 1955 season and all were scrapped after closure.

23/24
In 1946, the L&CBER acquired its final 'new' trams in the guise of two second-hand cars from Darwen Corporation. Originally Nos 24 and 23 respectively, Nos 23 and 24 were originally built by English Electric in 1936/37 on English Electric-built maximum traction bogies. Regauged from 4ft to 3ft 6in before entering service in North Wales, the two trams were not perhaps as successful as L&CBER expected and were restricted in their operation. The two were last operated in 1953 but not scrapped until after closure.

23A
Also acquired from Bournemouth in 1936 was No 23A; this was originally new to Poole & District Tramways Co Ltd in 1901 as No 1, becoming Bournemouth Corporation No 55 four years later. Rebuilt as a railgrinder in 1921, it was to serve as a works car on the L&CBER until closure.

No 12, seen at West Shore, was one of ten trams acquired from Bournemouth in 1936. This had been No 128 on the south coast and was new in 1927. *R.W.A. Jones/ Online Transport Archive*

Only three of the line's original trams remained in service post-war – Nos 16-18. Here No 17 is seen picking up passengers at St Paul's. Note the use of double trolleys. These were a later addition when the cars were modified and fitted with less powerful motors. *Jones/Online Transport Archive*

One of the quartet of open-top toast-rack cars, No 20, heads towards Colwyn Bay along Penrhyn Avenue at the Church Road crossroads. *R.W.A. Jones/Online Transport Archive*

Undoubtedly the most modern 4ft 0in gauge trams built, Darwen Nos 23 and 24 were to have their numbers switched when converted to operate on the 3ft 6in gauge L&CBER. Here No 24 stands outside the depot at Rhos-on-Sea. *R.W.A. Jones/ Online Transport Archive*

No 23A had been converted to a railgrinder by Bournemouth Corporation in 1921; the L&CBER acquired the tram for works duties in 1936. *R.W.A. Jones/Online Transport Archive*

LUAS

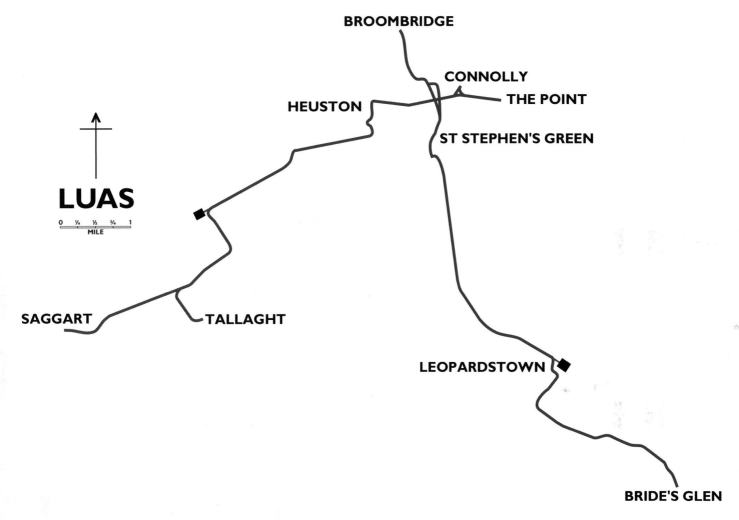

BROOMBRIDGE

CONNOLLY

THE POINT

HEUSTON

ST STEPHEN'S GREEN

LUAS

0   ¼   ½   ¾   1
MILE

SAGGART   TALLAGHT

LEOPARDSTOWN

BRIDE'S GLEN

Following studies in the early 1970s, plans were drawn up for the development of the railway network around Dublin and, as the first phase of this, the electrification of the Howth to Bray line was approved at the end of 1979. The line – branded as the Dublin Area Rapid Transit – commenced operation on 23 July 1984. However, the costs meant that the Irish government was slow to sanction the other extensions to Greystones and Malahide and extra trains.

In the early 1990s, proposals for a new light rail network emerged and, in 1994, the government asks CIÉ to develop a two-phase network – from Tallaght to Dundrum as phase 1 and Ballymum to the city centre and Dundrum to Sandyford as phase 2. Powers for CIÉ to operate a light-rail network were enshrined in the Transport (Dublin Light Rail) Act of 1996 but, before construction commenced, there were a number of amendments to the planned routes.

Construction commenced, following earlier pre-construction work, in March 2001 on the Tallaght to Connolly and Sandyford to St Stephen's Green sections; the section from St Stephen's Green to the airport was dropped. Work on the construction was led by the Italian company Ansaldo and the Australian MVM. May 2001 saw the unveiling of the first Luas (Irish for speed) tram in London

One of the '30xx' series of French-built articulated trams recorded at the Connolly terminus in 2005, shortly after the Red Line opened. *Martin Jenkins/Online Transport Archive*

St Stephen's Green to Sandyford (Ath an Ghainimh) was the first section of the LUAS system to open. One of the fourteen '40xx' series articulated trams is seen at the northern terminus in 2005. *Martin Jenkins/Online Transport Archive*

at a UITP conference held at Earl's Court; it was to be publicly launched in Dublin six months later. July 2001 saw the completion of the depot at Red Cow, for use on the Red Line, and in October that at Sandyford, for the Green Line, was also completed.

Following the completion of testing, the Green Line from Sandyford to St Stephen's Green opened on 30 June 2004; the Red Line, from Tallaght to Connolly, followed on 26 September the same year. Since these lines were completed, there have been a number of extensions: Connolly to the Docklands (The Point) on 8 December 2009; Sandyford to Bride's Glen on 16 October 2010; and, Belgard to Saggart on 2 July 2011. This took the system to 24km in total and a number of further extensions are either under construction or planned. The most notable of these is the northern extension of the Green Line from St Stephen's Green, through the city centre (crossing the Red Line) to Broombridge. Construction on this line commenced in June 2013 and passenger services were introduced on 9 December 2017.

DEPOTS

There are currently three depots serving the Luas system. On the Green Line, there is a depot at Sandyford, which can accommodate thirty-two units, whilst on the Red Line there is one at Red Cow, which can accommodate forty-seven, to the west of the station of the same name. These depots effectively opened contemporaneously with the launch of the services on the two routes; that at Red Cow was commissioned for test running in early 2002 whilst that at Sandyford followed in early 2003. The third depot is situated close to the Broombridge terminus and opened with the line.

OPENINGS

30 June 2004	St Stephen's Green to Sandyford
26 September 2004	Tallaght to Connolly
8 December 2009	Connolly to The Point
16 October 2010	Sandyford to Bride's Glen
2 July 2011	Belgard to Saggart
9 December 2017	St Stephen's Green to Broombridge

For the opening of the Red Line, from Connolly to Tallaght, twenty-six three-section articulated cars, such as No 3010 seen here in 2005, were supplied. The 30m-long vehicles have subsequently been lengthened to 40m. *Martin Jenkins/ Online Transport Archive*

No 4009, one of 14 trams initially supplied for the Green Line in 2004, heads towards Connolly at the Red Line's Belgard stop. This stop is at the junction of the Tallaght and Saggart lines and features an interesting fabric canopy over the platforms. *Donal Murray*

FLEET

3001-26

Two batches of trams were ordered from the French manufacturer Alstom for the opening of the line. This batch, constructed like the other two, at the company's La Rochelle factory, were originally 30m long Citadis 301 articulated cars. The first car was initially displayed in London in May 2001 at the UITP conference before reaching Dublin in October 2001. The trams entered service with the opening of the line on 26 September 2004. This batch was designated for use on the Red Line. Between early 2007 and June 2008, the trams were extended to 40m in length by the insertion of two further articulated sections.

4001-14

The other cars ordered for the system's opening were fourteen Citadis 401 40m-long articulated cars for use on the Green Line. These entered service on 30 June 2004. Following the introduction of the '5000' series of trams, the '4000' series cars were transferred to the Red Line.

5001-26

A total of twenty-six Citadis 402 43m-long cars were ordered from Alstom for delivery in 2009; these are fully low-floor and, at

No 5017 is pictured on the approach ramp from Peter Place to Charlemont Bridge and Luas stop; this, in turn, leads directly onto the old Harcourt Street Line alignment. No 5017 was one of 26 delivered in 2009 with a further 10 due for delivery for the Broombridge extension. *Donal Murray*

present, are used exclusively on the Green Line. In order to supplement the service for the Green Line extension across the Liffey to Broombridge, a further batch of Citadis 502 cars was ordered in November 2015.

These new cars are virtually identical to the '402' type and the first was delivered in late 2017. At 55m in length, the nine-section cars, Nos 5027-34, are amongst the longest trams in the world.

MANX ELECTRIC RAILWAY

During the summer of 1958 'Paddlebox' No 27 stands at Ramsey whilst passengers board. *F.K. Farrell/Online Transport Archive*

Following the nationalisation of the MER in 1957, a number of trams were repainted in a new green and white livery. No 29 is seen here in May 1961 carrying the short-lived – and unpopular – livery. *W. J. Wyse/LRTA (London Area) Collection/Online Transport Archive*

On 16 May 1970, MER No 2 is seen at Laxey; in the foreground is closed wagon No 16. Alongside the passenger service, the MER also operated freight and mail trains and, for that purpose, employed a number of wagons. At its peak in the 1920s, the line's wagon stock numbered twenty-six but only a handful still survive. No 16 was one of closed wagons – the last constructed for the line – built in the railway's own workshops in 1908 designed for use with the mail. No 16 was to be withdrawn in the late 1970s and was subsequently salvaged; it was fully restored in 2015. It was the loss of the mail traffic in the mid-1970s that was one of the threats to the future of the Laxey to Ramsey section. *Barry Cross Collection/Online Transport Archive*

On 17 September 2000 Manx Electric Railway No 21 enters Laxey with a service from Ramsey to Douglas. Alongside are Snaefell Nos 1 and 3; the latter was to be destroyed following a derailment in March 2016. *Author*

The MER emerged from the Second World War with a fleet of some fifty-two trams and trailers and some initial optimism as tourist traffic was strong – some 750,000 passengers being carried annually in the years after the war – and the line benefited from fuel restrictions that restricted coach competition. This was not, however, to last as the company's finances became increasingly stretched and as coach competition grew.

The declining financial position led for the first time to no winter service being operated over the line during the winter of 1951/52. In 1954, the Manx parliament sanctioned an increase in fares to a maximum of 3d per mile, however, an application to suspend winter services entirely, which was estimated to save £3,638 annually, was rejected. At the end of 1955, the MER board announced that, without financial support, the line would close completely at the end of the 1956 season. Although the line had made a profit that year – its first since 1952 – the annual accounts showed arrears of £22,974 to the debenture holders. The company was prepared, however, to sell the line to the government for £70,000.

As a result of the board's pronouncement, Tynwald instructed the Isle of Man Tourist Board on 22 January 1956 to examine proposals for the line's future whilst a sub-committee of Tynwald was established to examine the subject. British Railways was approached to produce a report; this asserted that the retention of the line would cost £674,000 – for track and vehicle replacement – and advocated that the line be abandoned in favour of bus operation. A second group reported more favourably, highlighting the historic value of the route and noting that the capital costs could be spread over a number of years.

Although the sub-committee accepted BR's recommendations, this was rejected by Tynwald on 20 June 1956. Following further discussions, the sub-committee recommended on 21 November 1956

that the government acquire the line for the agreed – but reduced – price of £50,000 (effectively the scrap price). This was debated and agreed in Tynwald on 12 December 1956. The bill authorizing the purchase of the line was passed in April 1957 and, on 1 June 1957, ownership of the MER and Snaefell Mountain Railway passed to the new Manx Electric Railway Board. The original company passed into receivership. The line's change of ownership was reflected in a change of livery; green and white appeared in place of the traditional colours. This proved unpopular and was relatively short-lived.

The change of ownership did not bring an immediate change of fortune, however; originally Tynwald had expected a subsidy of £25,000 per annum to suffice. The new board required more and sought a further £20,000; when this was rejected, all bar one of the new directors resigned. Opposition to the retention of the entire tramway was strong in Tynwald and a motion arguing for closure north of Laxey was only narrowly defeated. The new board accepted the figure of £25,000 but reduced the rate of reconstruction.

Work on the line's rebuilding progressed with the result that, by 1962, more than half of the track had been relaid and much of the overhead replaced by new grooved wire. The board also took advantage of tramway abandonment in Britain to acquire twelve compressors from Sheffield in November 1960 and four from Glasgow two years later. During the winter of 1963/64, the station facilities at Douglas and Ramsey were upgraded whilst, by the end of 1964, all the substations were automated and, with the exception of that at Laxey, were unstaffed. Improved financial results during these years allowed some of the subsidy to be diverted to fund capital expenditure.

In 1963, the Manx government combined the annual £25,000 subsidy and additional grant for capital work, designed to alleviate unemployment, into a single payment. That the line's position remained precarious was highlighted by the £32,000 loss made in 1963, although that was exacerbated by the poor weather during the season, which reduced passenger traffic. Although the reconstruction of the Douglas to Laxey section was largely completed by 1965, the future of the line beyond Laxey remained in doubt. In early 1966 a report by the Transport Committee to Tynwald in early 1966 highlighted these doubts. The problem was about to get worse; on 23 January 1967, a section of the line at Bulgham Bay collapsed, severing the Laxey to Ramsey section. Services were operated both north and south of the breach whilst repair work was undertaken with passengers walking around the gap. It was not until 10 July 1967 that through services were restored.

The threat to the northern section of the line became a reality in the mid-1970s. Following the loss of the Post Office contract in October 1975, services between Laxey and Ramsey were suspended and were not reinstated the following year. This closure, combined with the threat to the remaining section of the Isle of Man Railway, led to transport being a major issue in the 1976 Tynwald elections. The result was that the Ramsey section reopened for the 1977 summer service with the MER and Isle of Man Railway being amalgamated under the name of the Isle of Man Railways in order to improve co-ordination and marketing. A further change of ownership occurred in 1983 when the Isle of Man Passenger Transport Board was created.

A long-term commitment to the line was given by Tynwald on 16 November 1983 when it agreed unanimously that the line would remain open 'for such period as the Board may determine in accordance with the Board's statutory powers'. Tynwald accepted the proposer's assertion that the constant five-year reviews to the line's future made long-term planning impossible. Elsewhere, following opposition, the Church Commissioners decided against building a new vicarage at Laxey on part of the station site. The board was to survive until 1986,

when control of the MER passed to the Manx government's Department of Tourism and Transport; this body – now known as the Department of Community, Culture and Leisure – retains overall control.

For the next decade, there were two main aspects to the development of the line. The first of these was the ongoing programme of work to upgrade the route. A rebuilt station at Ballasalla was, for example, opened formally on 5 April 1986, whilst the same year witnessed the repainting of traction columns in traditional green rather than the grey or black that they had been painted in more recently. Towards the end of the 1980s, a new 11kV feeder cable was installed to replace the original 1903 underground cable at Groudle, whilst it was also planned to replace the substation at Ballaglass with one at Ballagorry. 1988 saw a new passenger shelter completed at Lewaigue.

The other facet was the increasing number of special events launched to try and attract the crowds to visit the island and travel on its historic transport. From the centenary of the first section of the Isle of Man Railway in 1979 – for which MER Nos 32 and 62 had been repainted in the unpopular 1957 green livery (they reverted to standard livery in 1986) – a number of these events were held. These resulted in the unusual spectacle of, for example, the Ramsey Pier diesel train operating over the MER following a successful test run from Ramsey to Walpole Drive on 22 October 1984 and steam on the MER in 1993 when No 4 *Loch* was used on several occasions during the year.

The winter of 1995/96 was particularly harsh; as result a number of roads were closed and the MER ran additional services, over and above the usual winter service, for a period to help transport schoolchildren and those commuting to or from work. During the summer of 1996 an ex-Lisbon tram – No 360 built by John Stephenson Co in 1907 – was acquired with a view to its use on the line. In the event it was found to be too wide and, after a period of storage, its body was used as a shelter between 2000 and 2002. After a further period of storage, the body was sold in 2009 and again in 2013. It is still extant but now privately owned.

The service pattern was varied during the winter of 1999/2000 when, for the first time for a number of years, a Saturday and Sunday service was operated from 1 November through to 19 December 1999. In previous years, the winter service had been limited to weekdays only. Between 1999 and 2003 half the MER's track was relaid and this programme of ongoing work has continued subsequently; a further £750,000 was granted in late 2002 for additional track work. That there was an ongoing need for maintenance was demonstrated on 20 October 2002 when the line faced a number of landslips following heavy rain. Services were suspended between Ramsey and Laxey whilst repairs were undertaken; the line was fully reopened on 24 October. In April 2003 David Cretney, the then Minister of Tourism, announced a conservation project for both the MER and Snaefell, reflecting the importance historically of the two lines. Over the winter of 2005/06, the Summerland complex adjacent to the Derby castle terminus was demolished; this resulted in the MER not operating a winter service – the first time that this had been suspended for a number of years.

Today, the MER continues to function; it has benefited from significant investment in its infrastructure and to the care of its surviving fleet with regular special events helping to boost the line's revenues.

DEPOTS

The MER had three depots. That at Derby Castle opened with the line to Groudle Glen on 7 September 1893 but has undergone modernisation over the years, including a significant rebuilding in the late 1990s when the old top shed was demolished in 1997 and replaced by a new structure. When the line opened to Laxey on 23 July 1894, a second depot was

completed. This was to be destroyed by fire in April 1930 and was subsequently rebuilt. A temporary depot was operated at Ballure following the opening of the line north from Laxey on 5 August 1898 but this was to close when the route was completed through to Ramsey on 24 July 1899. The line's third depot was located slightly to the south of the terminus at Ramsey; the depot with its associated good shed was demolished in December 2016.

FLEET

All the postwar fleet is still in service or in store (split between Laxey and Derby Castle depots) with the operator at the time of writing; not all those in store are in an operable condition. All the fleet is single deck.

1/2

For the opening of the first section of the line in 1893 G. F. Milnes & Co of Birkenhead supplied three unvestibuled bogie cars, Nos 1-3, fitted with Brush D bogies. One of the trio, No 3, was one of the trams destroyed in the fire at Laxey shed in 1930. The remaining two cars, following a period when they were used primarily for works duties, were restored to original condition in 1979. Both are currently operational.

5/6/7/9

For the extension to Laxey in 1894 G.F. Milnes supplied a further six bogie cars – Nos 4-9 – which were vestibuled from new and completed with Brush D bogies. As a result of their longitudinal seating these trams became known as the 'Tunnel' cars. Two of the sextet – Nos 4 and 8 – were victims of the 1930 Laxey fire and No 7 was, like Nos 1 and 2, largely relegated to works duties for a period before undergoing a comprehensive restoration in 2010. In 1993, No 9 was converted into an illuminated car. All are currently operational.

14-18

The fourth batch of cars supplied to the line were five crossbench cars,

MER No 2 was one of three trams supplied in 1893 for the opening of the first section of the line; it is seen here inside the depot at Laxey on 9 April 1950. Note the ladder carried on the side; this was needed when the car was used by the overhead line department for work duties. *Tony Wickens/Online Transport Archive*

Six additional cars – Nos 4-9 – were supplied in 1894. Four survived post-war, including No 5 pictured here. *Phil Tatt/Online Transport Archive*

One of the quintet of crossbench cars supplied in 1898, No 18, stands at Derby Castle on 10 August 1947. *John Meredith/Online Transport Archive*

Nos 14-18. All bar No 16, which has Brush D bogies, were fitted with Milnes S3 bogies. These were again built by G. F. Milnes & Co and delivered in 1898. Two – Nos 16 and 18 – are part of the operational fleet; the remaining three are in store. No 17 was slightly damaged in the fire in 1990 that resulted in the loss of No 22. No 16 is currently operational with No 14 undergoing restoration.

19-22

These four vestibuled cars, known as 'Winter Saloons', were built by G.F. Milnes & Co and delivered in 1899 in readiness for the opening of the section from Laxey to Ramsey. All are fitted with Brill 27Cx bogies. In 1990, the body of No 22 was largely destroyed by a fire at Derby Castle; the tram was, however, completely rebuilt to its original style but is now generally seen as a replica rather than an original car. No 19 was also slightly damaged in the same fire. All are currently operational.

23

Originally constructed as an electric locomotive by the Isle of Man Tramways & Electric Power Co Ltd in 1900, No 23 was eventually rebuilt during 1925 and 1926 with open wagon bodies at either end. Prior to withdrawal in 1993, the car generally operated using the Brill 27Cx bogies 'borrowed' from either No 32 or No 33. Following withdrawal, the car was preserved and is currently in store.

MER No 21, one of the four vestibuled 'Winter Saloons' built in 1899, departs from Laxey towards Douglas over the small viaduct south of the station. *Phil Tatt/Online Transport Archive*

MER No 23 was rebuilt from an electric locomotive into the form illustrated here in the mid-1920s. On withdrawal, the vehicle was to be preserved. *R.B. Parr/ NTM*

25-27

Delivered in 1898 and built by G.F. Milnes & Co, Nos 24-27, known as 'Paddleboxes' as a result of their unusual footboards, are unvestibuled crossbench cars. When delivered, the quartet were numbered 19-22 and were unpowered trailers. Renumbered 40-41 in 1899, the quartet were again renumbered as 24-27 in 1903, when they received new Brush D trucks to operate as motor cars. No 24 was one of the cars destroyed in the fire at Laxey in 1930. In 2003, No 25, not having operated since 1998, lost its bogies and motors; these were transferred to No 34. No 27 was fitted with rudimentary vestibule ends and operated from 1986 as a works car until 2003; it is now stored. No 26 has been out of service for a number of years.

28-31

In 1904, for its next batch of trams, the company changed supplier, opting for ERTCW of Preston to supply four unvestibuled crossbench cars on Milnes S3 bogies. All are extant but have not been used for some years in service and are currently stored in varying conditions: No 28 from 1970; No 29 from 1979; No 30 from 1971; and, No 31 from 2002.

32/33

A further two unvestibuled crossbench cars were supplied in 1906. These were built by UEC of Preston and fitted with Brill 27Cx bogies. When new, these cars, the most powerful built to operate over the line, were designed to be capable of hauling two trailers although this was rarely required in practice. Both are currently operational.

One of the 'Paddleboxes' delivered in 1898, No 26 is still based on the MER but, at the time of writing, has been out of service for a number of years. *Barry Cross Collection/Online Transport Archive*

MER No 28 was one of a batch of four supplied in 1904; like No 26, these four cars are still based on the line but have not been used for some years in service. *Barry Cross Collection/Online Transport Archive*

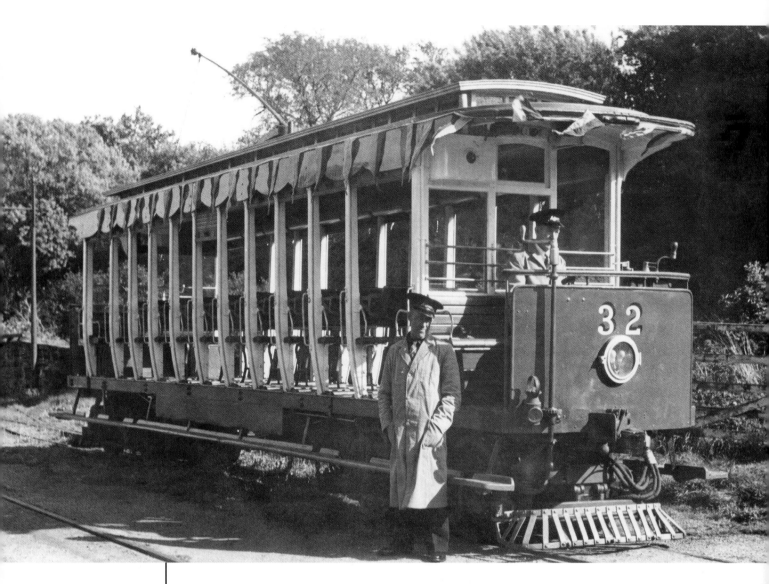

MER No 32 was one of two crossbench cars supplied by UEC in 1906; both remain in service. *Barry Cross Collection/Online Transport Archive*

34

In 1994, the MER constructed at Derby Castle a replica of SMR works car No 7; this was not successful and it was transferred to the MER. Regauged from 3ft 6in to 3ft 0in and now utilising the Brush D bogies and motors from No 25, the car is fitted with a diesel generator so that it can be operated independently of the overhead. It is currently in store.

36/37

G.F. Milnes & Co supplied six crossbench trailers with unpowered Milnes S2 bogies, Nos 17-22, for the line's opening from Groudle Glen to Laxey in 1894; as the fleet grew, the sextet were renumbered 34-39 in 1898. Four of the

sextet – Nos 34, 35, 38 and 39 – were destroyed in the Laxey fire of 1930. Of the remaining two, No 37 was used with Nos 1 or 2 to form the line's vintage set for a period but in 2009 was found to be suffering from cracked axles and so was taken out of service. It remains in store at Derby Castle. No 36, effectively withdrawn at the end of the 1971 season, is stored at Derby Castle as is No 37.

40/41/44

In 1930, a number of trams were destroyed in a disastrous depot fire at Laxey; whilst none of the motor cars were replaced, three replacement crossbench trailer cars – Nos 40/41/44 – were constructed by English Electric at Preston in 1930. All three are

No 36 was one of six crossbench trailers supplied by G.F. Milnes & Co in 1894. Four were destroyed in the disastrous fire at Laxey in 1930; No 36, although still with the railway, has not been in service since the early 1970s. *Barry Cross Collection/Online Transport Archive*

Trailer No 40, one of three replacement trailer cars constructed after the disastrous depot fire of 1930, pictured at Ramsey on 17 September 2000. *Author*

fitted with unpowered Milnes S1 bogies that were salvaged from the trailers destroyed in the 1930 fire. All are currently operational.

42/43

These two crossbench trailers were built by G.F. Milnes & Co of Birkenhead and delivered, fitted with unpowered Milnes S3 bogies, in 1903. Whilst No 42 is currently in store No 43 is operational.

45-48

In 1899, Milnes supplied four crossbench trailers; these were fitted with either Milnes S1 or S2 unpowered bogies. All are still extant and remain serviceable although No 45 lost its body in 2003 when converted into a flat wagon for use as a works car. All are currently operational.

49-54

For the opening of the line from Douglas to Groudle Glen in 1893, G.F. Milnes & Co supplied six lightweight trailers on unpowered Milnes bogies. When delivered, these were originally numbered 11-16, becoming Nos 23-28 in 1895. A further renumbering during 1903 and 1904 saw the sextet become Nos 49-54. No 52 was used, with its seat and roof removed, as a permanent way flat wagon for a number of years; this arrangement was made permanent in 1954 when its body was scrapped. In 1987 No 51 was restored to its original – 'Umbrella' – condition and renumbered back to 13; it re-entered service in this new guise on 23 May 1987. It reverted to No 51 in 2001; this car remains in service whilst the other four are in store.

In 1903 G.F. Milnes supplied two crossbench trailers; one of the duo – No 42 – is seen at Douglas Castle in the company of No 19 on 18 September 2000. *Author*

No 46, pictured at Derby Castle on 10 August 1947, was one of four crossbench trailers supplied by G.F. Milnes in 1899. *John Meredith/Online Transport Archive*

Also recorded at Derby Castle on 10 August 1947, was trailer No 49. This was one of six supplied for the line's opening in 1893. *John Meredith/Online Transport Archive*

Crossbench trailer
No 55 was one
of two supplied
by ERTCW in
1904. *Barry Cross
Collection/Online
Transport Archive*

55/56
The Preston-based ERTCW supplied two trailers, Nos 55 and 56, in 1904, fitted with Brill 27Cx unpowered bogies. Between 1994 and 1999, No 56 was modified to become the line's sole vehicle offering complete disabled access. It is fitted with, inter alia, hydraulic wheelchair ramps. It remains operational although No 55 is in store.

57/58
Constructed by ERTCW in 1904, these unvestibuled enclosed saloon trailers are fitted with Brill 27Cx bogies. Designed for use as winter cars, the two are less frequently used than the crossbench cars. However, they have been used for a number of special events, such as the 'Steam on Electric' specials operated in 1993 to mark the line's centenary when

Isle of Man Railway No 4 *Loch* was used to haul steam services between Laxey and Dhoon Quarry Halt with Nos 57/58 providing the coaching stock. Both are currently operational.

59
This unvestibuled but enclosed trailer was supplied as a one-off by G.F. Milnes & Co in 1895. Normally seating eighteen, the car is fitted with unpowered Milnes S2 bogies. Following its use by Queen Victoria during a royal visit, the trailer has become known as the 'Royal Saloon'. It is rarely used in public service and spent some years on display at the Douglas terminus. It is currently in store.

60
No 60 is another one-off crossbench trailer supplied by G.F. Milnes & Co, this

On a particularly damp day, enclosed trailer No 57 stands at Derby Castle; this was one of two again supplied by ERTCW in 1904. *Phil Tatt/ Online Transport Archive*

Regarded as the 'Royal Saloon', following its use by Queen Victoria, No 59 is pictured inside the depot at Derby Castle on 15 August 1957. *John Meredith/Online Transport Archive*

Trailer No 60, originally built in 1896, is pictured outside Derby Castle depot on 29 May 1979. Alongside are the remains of Aachen tram No 1010; this was one of seven trams acquired following the closure of the German system. All of the trams were cannibalised in London but only one – No 1010 – made the trip to the Isle of Man. *R.L. Wilson/Online Transport Archive*

time in 1896. It is fitted with unpowered Milnes S1 bogies and, currently, normally operates with No 16. It is currently operational.

61/62
These two crossbench trailer cars were both supplied by UEC in 1906 and were designed to complement Nos 32 and 33. The two trailers were fitted with Brill 27CxT trucks. Although both trailers are extant, they are stored at Derby Castle having both been withdrawn in early 2009

following the discovery of cracked axles and are currently undergoing overhaul.

WORKS CARS AND GOODS WAGONS
The MER has employed a number of specialist works cars over the years; some are detailed above and are conversions from erstwhile passenger vehicles. Other dedicated works cars include a tower wagon, No 1 (built by G.F. Milnes & Co in 1894), which is still operational and tower van No 12 (built by G.F. Milnes in 1898 and currently undergoing restoration). Historically, the line also employed a number of freight wagons; although no commercial freight traffic is now carried a number of these survive, either in store, under restoration or fully restored.

Crossbench trailer No 61 stands at Laxey; in the distance is motor car No 33. Nos 32/33 and 61/62 were all supplied by UEC in 1906. *Phil Tatt/Online Transport Archive*

SNAEFELL MOUNTAIN RAILWAY

Snaefell Mountain Railway no 4 pictured at the Summit hotel. When the line was opened in 1895 a simple wooden structure was built for passengers. Very quickly as passenger traffic increased, this basic structure proved insufficient and so a new stone-built castellated structure was completed in 1902. This is the building featured in this view; however, this was to be destroyed by fire in 1982 and it was not until 1984 that a replacement building was completed. *Barry Cross Collection/Online Transport Archive*

As with the MER, following the nationalisation of the Snaefell Mountain Railway in 1957, the line's traditional livery – visible on No 3 in the background – was replaced briefly by the unpopular green and white livery carried by No 2, seen here at Laxey on 2 May 1961. The new livery had disappeared by 1963. *W.J. Wyse/ LRTA (London Area) Collection/Online Transport Archive*

On 21 September 1974, No 6 is seen ascending towards the summit from No 1 descending. *Barry Cross Collection/ Online Transport Archive*

In glorious later summer sunshine, Snaefell No 1 is seen at the summit on 22 September 2000. *Author*

The Snaefell Mountain Railway, as a subsidiary of the MER, has a common history with that of its parent through to the take-over on 1 June 1957 by the Manx government. It has operated as a tourist attraction during the summer season annually; the only time a winter operation was undertaken in its history was during the early 1950s when the line was kept open when the Air Ministry used the railway to facilitate the construction of a new radar station.

As a summer operation only, the line had last operated on 20 September 1939; it was not until 1 June 1946 that services were restored post-war. Before services could be reinstated, the overhead on the upper section – removed for storage early in the war – had to be restored whilst each of the passenger cars had to undergo maintenance, for which they were taken to Derby Castle. The Air Ministry established a radar station on Snaefell in 1950; the annual removal of the upper section overhead each winter resulted in the arrival

of the first Wickham railcar the following year so that the Air Ministry could access the summit during the winter months.

Following nationalisation in 1957, two of the trams – Nos 2 and 4 – were repainted in a new green and white livery similar to that adopted for a number of trams on the MER. This scheme was, however, hugely unpopular and the two trams reverted to their traditional livery. Shortly after the line's nationalisation, the Bungalow Hotel was closed. It was subsequently demolished. During the 1960s, a certain amount of work on the line was undertaken; this included replacement of the Fell – middle – rail along the entire route in 1968 and the following winters saw the running rails relaid. The Summit Hotel was also refurbished during the decade.

For the bulk of the period, the line has been operated by the six original tramcars supplied by G.F. Milnes & Co for its opening in 1895. However, two of these have now been destroyed. On 16 August 1970, No 5 was destroyed by fire; the MER constructed a replica vehicle using the original trucks and underframe. This tram was distinguishable from the other five by the absence of a clerestroy roof and the use of aluminium window frames; this remained the case until a further rebuild in 2003 when wooden frames were installed. On 30 March 2016, No 3 was written off when it ran away from the Summit and derailed just north of Bungalow station, fortunately without any loss of life or injury. At the time of writing, the remains of the tram are in store although it is expected that a second replica will be completed eventually.

By the mid-1970s, there was increasing concern about the condition of reliability of the trams. As a result, a party from the MER board and two London Transport engineers visited Aachen with a view to acquiring equipment that could be used to replace the life-expired parts on the fleet. The Aachen tram system had finally closed on 29 September 1984 and the operator was looking to dispose of its fleet. In 1957, the Aachen-based manufacturer Waggonfabrik Talbot & Co had supplied eleven four-axle trams, and these were deemed to be suitable donor vehicles. As a result, seven were acquired – Nos 1003-05/08-11 – and shipped to London for the parts to be removed and the remains of six to be scrapped. The first of the Snaefell fleet to be treated was No 1; its trucks went to London during the winter of 1976/77 for use as templates. Replacement trucks using the ex-Aachen motors were completed and returned to the island. The success of the work resulted in the remaining five cars being similarly treated: Nos 2 and 3 during the winter of 1977/78 and Nos 4-6 during the winter of 1978/79. In theory, the seventh ex-Aachen car, No 1010, was to be sent to the Isle of Man with a spare set of equipment; however, whilst the tram arrived, its equipment did not. The remains of the tram were subsequently scrapped.

In 1982, fire gutted the Summit Hotel; due to its remoteness and problems in getting the emergency services to the site, the building was virtually destroyed. It was to remain closed for almost two years. In the summer of 1983, work commenced on its reconstruction, with building materials transported using the line and the siding at Bungalow. The new facility was formally opened on 7 May 1984. Further work was undertaken in 1985 but it was not until 2011 that a significant upgrade commenced.

The increased use of electric braking resulted in some modification to the trackwork. To prevent rail creep, the late 1980s witnessed the installation of rail anchors on the down line whilst the Fell rail through the complex pointwork to the depot at Laxey was removed. This was due to problems with expansion and rail creep, which had resulted in the Fell rail becoming inoperable. On 4 August 2017, one of the surviving trams suffered a fault on its braking system that led it to miss the stop at Bungalow. Investigation suggested that this was the result the failure of the normal electric braking system. Usually, under these circumstances, the crew would use the Fell system to stop the tram; however, the location of the incident – the road crossing at Bungalow – meant that the Fell rail was not present. Once the Fell rail was regained, the tram was brought to a safe stop. This incident resulted in the imposition of new speed restrictions (8mph rather than 12mph with a consequent reduction in service frequency); however, the failure to comply with these on a number of occasions resulted in the Health & Safety at Work Executive on the island forcing the suspension of services on 10 August; following further testing, services were resumed on the following day. On 25 September, services were again suspended – effectively for the remainder of the summer season – whilst further investigative and remedial work was undertaken; in the period leading up to the second suspension, the frequency of service had been much reduced and on some days no trams had operated at all.

As with the MER control of the line passed to the Manx Department of Tourism and Transport in 1986; this is now the Department of Community, Culture and Leisure. Now more than 120 years old,

Two of the original Snaefell cars have been destroyed in accidents, most recently No 3 in March 2016. In happier days, No 3 is pictured at Laxey on 19 September 2000. *Author*

the line continues to provide a seasonal service to the top of Snaefell.

DEPOT
There is a single depot to accommodate the Snaefell fleet; this is situated at Laxey and opened formally with the line itself on 21 August 1895. It was extended slightly at the rear in late 1992. A second smaller facility is also located at Laxey; this houses the Wickham trolley utilised by National Air Traffic Services for the maintenance of the aerial masts on the upper section when the overhead is removed over the winter to prevent frost damage.

1-6
To operate the line, six 3ft 6in gauge single-deck cars were acquired from G.F. Milnes & Co in 1895; these were all supplied with bogies from the same manufacturer. The fleet was to remain intact until 16 October 1970 when No 5 was burnt out. The five underwent retrucking during the late 1970s using equipment salvaged from redundant Aachen trams; this resulted in the introduction of rheostatic braking and allowed for the elimination of the Fell

brakes. No 3 was written off in March 2016 following a derailment.

5 (II)
Following the destruction of the original No 5, a replica car was constructed by the MER on the original Milnes-built bogies; this entered service in 1971. The tram received replacement trucks, as with the remainder of the fleet, over the winter of 1978/79.

7
A seventh car – No 7 (and nicknamed *Maria*) – was also supplied in 1895. This was used for works purposes, including the movement of coal from Laxey to the power station. Lacking its own trucks, it used equipment from one of the passenger cars when required. It latterly stood at the depot resting on barrels until being scrapped. A replica was constructed in 1994; this was subsequently transferred to the MER (as No 34). In order to service the aerial masts, the Air Ministry introduced the first of a number of Wickham trolleys to the line in 1951. In all, the Air Ministry and its successors (the Civil Aviation Authority and the National Air Traffic Services) have employed four Wickham trolleys, the most recent of which was delivered in 1991.

In 1971, following the loss of the original car, a replica No 5 entered service; it is seen here at Laxey on 30 June 1993. *Les Folkard/Online Transport Archive*

The first of the Wickham-built trolleys used by the Air Ministry in connection with the aerial installation was No 1. This was Works No 5864 and arrived on the line in 1951. It is pictured here on 19 May 1956 in the RAF blue livery in which it was painted. No 1 survived until 1977 when it was transferred to the MER. It was sold for preservation in the UK in 2007. *M.J. Lea/LRTA (London Area) Collection/Online Transport Archive*

The remains of No 7, *Maria*, are pictured at Laxey on 21 September 1974. *Barry Cross Collection/Online Transport Archive*

On 19 May 1956 Snaefell No 3 is pictured outside the shed at Laxey; when destroyed by an accident in March 2016, No 3 was the second of the fleet of six to be lost in 120 years of operation. *M. K. Lea/ LRTA (London Area) Collection/Online Transport Archive*

SWANSEA & MUMBLES

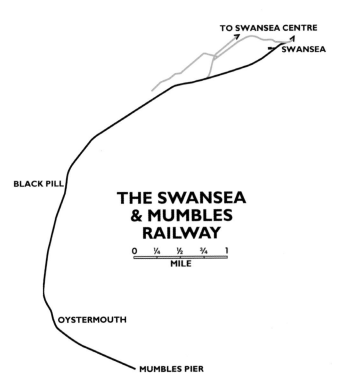

TO SWANSEA CENTRE

SWANSEA

BLACK PILL

**THE SWANSEA
& MUMBLES
RAILWAY**

0   ¼   ½   ¾   1
MILE

OYSTERMOUTH

MUMBLES PIER

Towards the end
of the tramway's
life, one of the 13
passenger trams –
No 3 – is pictured at
Mumbles Pier. *Frank
Hunt/LRTA (London
Area) Collection/
Online Transport
Archive*

As an expectant crowd waits, Swansea & Mumbles 10 and 8 wait at the Rutland Street terminus for loading to commence. *R.W.A Jones/Online Transport Archive*

The post-war era saw the Swansea & Mumbles in a relatively secure position; its status, enshrined in the Swansea & District Transport Act of 29 May 1936, was that the South Wales Transport Co Ltd operated the line under the terms of the 999-year lease granted by the Swansea & Mumbles Railway Ltd and the Mumbles Railway & Pier Co to the Swansea Improvements & Tramways Co of 1 July 1899 as transferred to South Wales Transport in January 1927.

In 1945, the line carried 5 million passengers although this dropped to 3 million in 1953; the decline was partly down to the temporary closure of Mumbles Pier for safety reasons in early 1953 (it was not to reopen until 9 June 1956). Although these passenger levels were still higher than those achieved before the war, the line's financial position was deteriorating.

However, before any serious threat to the line emerged, it was possible during June 1954 for the 150th anniversary of the Oystermouth Railway to be celebrated in some style. This culminated with a major event on 29 June when local schools were given a special day's holiday and there was a procession of vehicles, including a replica horse-drawn tram, accompanied

The last trams
to operate on the
Swansea & Mumbles
were Nos 6 and 7;
the pair, suitably
decorated, are
pictured approaching
Rutland Street in
a view that shows
to good effect
the proximity of
the Swansea &
Mumbles line to the
BR (ex-LNWR) line
heading west from
Swansea Victoria
station. *F.E.J. Ward/
Online Transport
Archive (FEJW1032)*

by staff and passengers in period costume.

The celebrations could not mask the serious condition that the line was in; the temporary closure of Mumbles Pier adversely affected passenger levels and, by the time of its reopening, the tramway was operating at a loss. Moreover, there was an urgent need to spend £350,000 to renew the track – money that simply was not available. As a bus operator primarily, South Wales Transport looked at the possibility of simply replacing the trams by buses; however, this would still have required the company to pay the leaseholders £14,242 per annum in rent.

It looked as though, for a period, that the impasse would ensure, by default, the tramway's survival. However, in September 1958, South Wales Transport made a formal offer to acquire the shares of the Swansea &

Mumbles Railway Ltd and the Mumbles Railway & Pier Co. The shareholders accepted the offer and so South Wales Transport was in a position to move forward with the tramway's abandonment. Even this was not straightforward as it required an Act of Parliament – the South Wales Transport Act of 29 July 1959 – to enable the tramway to be formally abandoned.

In order to progress the abandonment, the first closure occurred on 11 October 1959 when the section between Southend and Mumbles Pier was closed. This was to allow for the construction of a new private road to allow the replacement buses to reach the Pier terminus. The final services operated from Rutland Street to Southend on 5 January 1960. The last two cars – both suitably decorated – were Nos 6 and 7.

After closure, one of the cars – No 2 – was secured for preservation; based

The last of the Brush-built cars, No 13, stands at Southend; the section from Southend to Mumbles Pier was the first part of the line to close, in October 1959, to permit the construction of a private road for the replacement buses. *R.W.A Jones/Online Transport Archive*

Swansea & Mumbles No 3 was one of 13 massive double-deck cars supplied by Brush for the electrification of the line. *D. Kelk/ Online Transport Archive*

on the Middleton Railway near Leeds, it was one of a number of preserved trams at the site to be heavily vandalised and ultimately scrapped. The cab section of a second tram – No 7 – does, however, survive and is currently displayed in its home city alongside restored Swansea Improvements & Tramways Co No 14.

DEPOT

The Swansea & Mumbles employed a single depot during its life as an electric tramway. This was a two-road structure at Rutland Street in Swansea. This opened on 2 March 1929 and was to survive right through until the abandonment of the tramway on 5 January 1960.

CLOSURES

| 11 October 1959 | Southend to Mumbles Pier |
| 5 January 1960 | Swansea to Southend |

FLEET

1-13

In order to operate the newly electrified line, the Swansea & Mumbles acquired thirteen trams from Brush; No 1-11 were delivered in 1928 whilst Nos 12 and 13 came the following year. Fitted with Brush-built equal wheel bogies, each car could accommodate 106 seated passengers, making them amongst the largest first-generation electric tramcars to operate in Britain. As the passengers could only enter and exit from one side, the trams were also unusual in that entrances were only to the landward side. All thirteen survived until the system's closure in 1960. One of the cars, No 2, was preserved at closure and stored on the Middleton Railway in Leeds; damage from vandalism resulted, however, in its scrapping in the 1960s. The cab from a second car – No 7 – is on display at the Swansea Industrial & Maritime Museum.

16-18

These were three unpowered works cars. No 16 was a tower wagon, No 17 a ballast wagon and No 18 a weedkiller tank. All survived until the system's final closure in January 1960.

The interior of the lower deck on one of the 13 Brush-built trams supplied to operate the line on electrification; the cab section of one of the trams, No 7, is now preserved in Swansea, the only surviving part of any Swansea & Mumbles electric tram.
F. E. J. Ward/Online Transport Archive

PRESERVATION

Following the line's closure, Bessbrook & Newry No 2 was secured for preservation. It is pictured here outside the Mather & Platt factory in Manchester where it was housed until the mid-1950s. *F.E.J. Ward/Online Transport Archive*

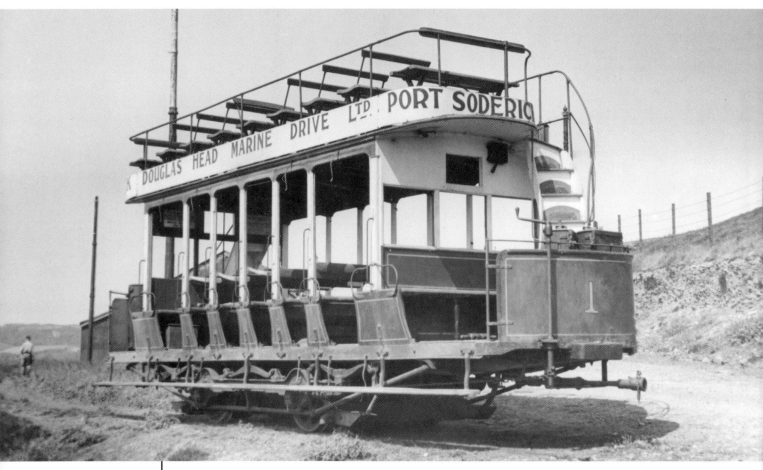

Following the cessation of operation of the Douglas Head Marine Drive in 1939, the fleet was stored in the depot until the early 1950s. When the assets of the line were disposed of No 1 was secured for preservation during the summer of 1951. The tram is seen here shortly after its removal from the depot and its transfer to England. It now forms part of the collection held by the National Tramway Museum. *D.W.K. Jones/National Tramway Museum*

The story of Dublin tram preservation is not a happy one; a number of trams that were secured in 1949 were subsequently vandalised and scrapped. More recently, however, the bodies of Nos 253 and 284 have been secured. Here No 284 is seen following acquisition at Castleruddery on 29 October 1977. *R. L. Wilson/Online Transport Archive*

One of the more remarkable survivors is the ex-Pwllheli Corporation horse tram; it is seen here on 24 May 1981 whilst is use as an information kiosk. *R.L. Wilson/Online Transport Archive*

The only Irish tram preserved as part of the National Tramway Museum collection is Hill of Howth No 10; now regauged to operate on 4ft 8½in, the tram was one of those loaned to Blackpool to mark that system's centenary. It is seen here at Talbot Square during the anniversary parade on 29 September 1985. *Michael H. Waller*

Looking first at Ireland, there are three trams that survive from Belfast. The oldest of these is horse tram No 118, which was new to the Belfast Street Tramways in 1885. Withdrawn in 1905, the body of the tram was rescued from use as a summer house at Monaghan in 1962 and restored. Two corporation trams, No 249, an open-top four-wheel car dating originally to 1905, and 'Chamberlain' No 357, built by Brush in 1930, were preserved when the system closed. All three are now on display in a non-operational condition at the Ulster Folk & Transport Museum at Cultra.

Also on display at Cultra are one of the four Hill of Howth cars to survive, No 4, and the sole surviving power car from the Bessbrook & Newry; this is the fully-enclosed single-deck No 2 that was originally built in 1885 but which was fitted with the body of Dublin & Lucan trailer No 24 in 1942. Cultra is also the home of the Great Northern Railway (I) horse car, No 381, which operated the Fintona branch from 1883 through to its closure in 1957. One of the two surviving 3ft 0in gauge steam tram engines built by Kitson & Co of Leeds for the Portstewart Tramway, No 2 of 1883, is also part of the collection at Cultra. A second Portstewart tram engine example, No 1 of 1882, is also preserved and is displayed at Hull's Streetlife Museum of Transport.

Finally, two of the three surviving trams from the Giant's Causeway tramway are also based at Cultra. These are the trailer cars No 2, which was built in Shrewsbury in 1883, and No 5, which also dates to 1883. The third Giant's Causeway trailer to survive is No 9, the motor car that was substantially rebuilt in 1945; this is currently under restoration by the Transport Museum Society of Ireland at its museum at Howth. Appropriately, the Howth museum is the home for the second Hill of Howth tram to survive in Ireland; this is No 9.

The TMSI also accommodates the three surviving ex-Dublin United Tramways Co cars; these are the two 'Standard Saloons' – Nos 253 and 284 – that dated originally to 1928. The body of the former is now restored but it lacks seats and bogies whilst the body of the latter awaits restoration. The third car to survive is the unique Directors' Car of 1901; following withdrawal, this was sold in 1950 and became a summer house at Dalkey. Seriously damaged by fire in 1984, the car's remains were transferred to Howth in August 1988 and it currently awaits restoration. There is notionally a fourth Dublin survival; this is No 224, which is also based at Howth. However, this body is in reality ex-London County Council trailer No T24, which was withdrawn in about 1922. Eventually, having spent some time converted to a horse-drawn caravan it ended up at a farm near Abbeyleix in County Laois. Preserved in September 1982, it was restored as a replica of a Dublin open-top car of 1900.

Two of the surviving trams from the Hill of Howth line are preserved outside Ireland; both have been converted to 4ft 8½in gauge to facilitate their operation. The National Tramway Museum at Crich owns No 10; this car operated at Blackpool between 1985 and 1989. No 2 is preserved in the USA, being based at the Orange Empire Railway Museum on California.

Turning to Wales, the National Tramway Museum at Crich is host to the two trams that survive from Cardiff. The oldest of these is Cardiff Tramways Co horse tram No 21, which was originally built by G.F. Milnes & Co in Birkenhead in 1890 and is now owned by the National Museum of Wales. It has been fully restored. The only ex-Cardiff electric tram to survive is No 131; this is a single-deck four-wheel works car that was originally built by ERTCW in 1902. Preserved on withdrawal in 1950, the car, which is unique now in being the only surviving purpose-built water car, was fully restored in 2007 and has subsequently been put to proper work in Blackpool when it was used for track cleaning in November 2011.

Apart from Cardiff No 21, a second Welsh horse tram survives; this is Pwllheli & Llanbedrog No 1, which was built originally by Brush in 1897. Withdrawn in 1927, the tram body spent 40 years in various uses before being rescued and converted into an information kiosk at Pwllheli in 1969. It was fully restored 1992 and is now on display at Llanbedrog.

A further historic vehicle rescued after many years is Neath gas tram No 1, which is now on display at the Cefn Coed Colliery Museum. The early history of the car is uncertain, but it passed to Neath Corporation in 1916 from the Provincial Gas Traction Co and was withdrawn in August 1920. Rescued for preservation in 1984, the car has been restored as a static exhibit.

Apart from the Cardiff works car, No 131, there are two electric passenger trams that operated in Wales which are still extant in complete condition. Displayed in Swansea is Swansea Improvement & Tramways Co No 14. Built by Brush in 1924, the tram was originally withdrawn in 1937 and its lower deck was rescued for preservation from a farm in Ammanford in 1977. Fully restored using the upper deck from No 12 united with a truck and equipment imported from Belgium, the car is displayed alongside a cab section of Swansea & Mumbles No 7. Following the destruction after vandalism and fire of complete Swansea & Mumbles No 2 in Leeds during the 1960s, this is the only part of a Swansea & Mumbles car to survive.

The second electric passenger car to survive is one of the ex-Bournemouth double-deck cars that operated on the Llandudno & Colwyn Bay Electric Railway. Bournemouth No 85 was sold to the L&CBER – as No 6 – in 1936 and was preserved on withdrawal in 1956. Now restored to Bournemouth condition, the car was displayed in its home town for a number of years but it has recently been transferred to the National Tramway Museum. Although neither were operated by the L&CBER, the bodies of two other Bournemouth trams – No 86 of 1914 and No 101 of 1921 – are owned by the Llandudno & Colwyn Bay Tramway Society. The latter's body has been restored as a L&CBER car whilst the society has the long-term ambition to restore No 86 to recreate an authentic operational L&CBER car.

Apart from these cars, the bodies of two Wrexham trams survive in the ownership of Wrexham County Borough Museum, although both are in poor condition and stored outside.

The position of the Isle of Man trams is complex as historically important cars represent the operational fleet of the three tramways on the island. The danger that this poses was demonstrated all too graphically in 2016, when one of the five surviving original cars from the Snaefell Mountain Railway was written off following an accident.

There are, however, a number of Manx trams that can be regarded as preserved rather than operational. The National Tramway Museum at Crich is home to the only car, No 1 from 1896, that survives from Douglas South Electric Tramways Ltd. This was built by Brush in 1896 and preserved in 1951. The Jurby Transport Museum houses the restored Douglas Corporation cable car No 72/73; this was withdrawn in 1929 and rescued for preservation in 1968. Now restored, it has been based at Jurby since 2010. Also based at Jurby is Douglas horse car No 22; this was new in 1890 and was used for more than thirty years as a tram shop before transfer to the museum in 2009.

The Manx Museum is home to Douglas Corporation double-deck horse tram No 14, which was built originally for South Shields in 1883 and was sold to Douglas in 1887. Stored in 1949, it was preserved six years later. One Douglas horse tram, No 46 from 1900, is currently in Edinburgh. Withdrawn in 1987 and displayed for a period at Birkenhead, No 46 has been largely dismantled to provide

At the time of writing, only one Douglas horse tram had been preserved in England. No 46, withdrawn in 1987, was based at Birkenhead until it was scrapped in 2001. *Harry Luff/ Online Transport Archive*

parts for the restoration of an Edinburgh horse tram. Three other horse trams are stored out of service on the island itself; these are No 11 of 1886, No 47 of 1911 and No 49 of 1935. Controversially, the Douglas fleet was significantly reduced when a number of cars were sold by auction in August 2016. The final location of these trams remains uncertain at the time of writing.

Of the Manx Electric fleet, all extant cars remain in the ownership of the Isle of Man government for operational purposes with the exception of works car No 23,

which dates to 1900, which is now owned by the Isle of Man Railway & Tramway Preservation Society and based at Laxey.

Finally, the body of one of the Guernsey electric trams, No 3, was rescued in 1976 after many years as a summer house. The body was restored and fitted to a chassis powered by an internal combustion engine; it was thus able to move under its own power and, in May 1980, it ran over the roads parallel to its original route. Still based on the island and now owned the government, the tram remains in long-term storage.

BIBLIOGRAPHY

CARMAN, W.J.: *100 Years of Public Transport: A Short History of the Guernsey Railway Co Ltd*; Guernsey Press; 1979.

COAKHAM, Desmond: *Tramway Memories: Belfast*; Ian Allan Publishing; 2005.

CORCORAN, Michael: *Through Streets Broad & Narrow: A History of Dublin n Trams*; Midland Publishing; 2000.

GABB, Gerald: *The Life and Times of the Swansea & Mumbles Railway,* D. Brown & Sons Ltd; 1987.

GOULD, David: *Cardiff's Electric Tramways*; Oakwood Press; 1996.

KILROY, James: *Irish Trams*; Colourpoint; 1996.

LEE, Charles E.: *The SSwansea & Mumbles Railway,* Oakwood Press; 1988.

MAYBIN, J.M.: *Belfast Corporation Tramways 1905-1954*; LRTA; undated.

MAYBIN, Mike: *A Nostalgic Look at Belfast Trams since 1945*; Silver Link; 1994.

McGUIGAN, J.H.: *The Giant's Causeway Tramway,* Oakwood Press; 1964.

RUSH, R.W.: *Horse Trams of the British Isles*; Oakwood Press; 2004.

TURNER, Keith, SMITH, Shirley and SMITH, Paul: *The Directory of British Tram Depots*; OPC; 2001.

TURNER, Keith: *The LLlandudno & Colwyn Bay Electric Railway,* Oakwood Press; 1993.

WALLER, Michael H. and WALLER, Peter: *British and Irish Tramway Systems since 1945*; Ian Allan Ltd; 1992.